"MARILYN,
ARE YOU SURE YOU CAN COOK?"
HE ASKED

"MARILYN, ARE YOU SURE YOU CAN COOK?" HE ASKED

A MEMOIR

MARILYN LEWIS

EDITED BY BRIGIT L. BINNS

TEN SPEED PRESS

BERKELEY TORONTO

To my mom, Ruth Laurette

Ten Speed Press
P.O. Box 7123
Berkeley, CA 94707
www.tenspeed.com

Distributed in Australia by Simon and Schuster Australia, in Canada by Ten Speed Press Canada, in New Zealand by Southern Publishers Group, in South Africa by Real Books, in Southeast Asia by Berkeley Books, and in the United Kingdom and Europe by Airlift Books.

Design by Campana Design
Unless otherwise noted, all photos from author's collection

Library of Congress Cataloging-in Publication Data
On file with the publisher
ISBN 1-58008-296-3
First printing, 2000
Printed in the United States of America

1 2 3 4 5 6 7 8 9 10 — 04 03 02 01 00

ACKNOWLEDGMENTS

To those who parted the sea and allowed the raw talent to find its way, we thank you for all those who know your name: Marion Christie, *The Boston Sunday Globe*; Fay Hammond, Mary Lou Loper, society editor, *Los Angeles Times*; Mary Lou Luther, fashion editor, *Los Angeles Times*; Patricia Shelton, *The Christian Science Monitor*; Jody Jacobs, *Women's Wear Daily*; Elizabeth Brady, fashion director, *Saks Fifth Avenue*; Eleanor Lambert of the Coty Awards; Eugenia Shepherd, Bernadine Morris, *New York Times*; Irv Kupcinet, *Chicago Sun Times*; Aaron Gold, *Chicago Tribune*; Bea Miller, *Life* magazine; Peg Zwecker, *Chicago Daily News*; Ann Gerber, Lerner Skyline, Barbara Molotsky, *Chicago Tribune*; Bess Winaker, *Chicago Sun Times*; Mary C. Jackson, *Sacramento Bee*; Pat Anderson, *Daily News*, Indio, California; Dorothy Neighbors, *The Seattle Times*; Julie Baumer, *The Desert Sun*; Mildred Meade, *The Newporter*; Blake Green, *San Francisco Chronicle*; Linda Glidewell, *Herald Examiner*; Bobbi McCallum, *Post Intelligencer*, *The New Yorker*, *Town and Country* magazine; Nancy Dinsmore, *Harpers Bazaar*; Eleanor Phillips, *Vogue* magazine; Anne Chamberlin, *Fortune* magazine; *The Washingtonian*; Dean Striner, American University; Arnold Lipkin, our CPA, who came to American University and taught the class "How to Read a Profit and Loss Statement"; Phil Grace, Washington, D.C.; *Palm Springs Life* magazine; Joan Kaiser, *Los Angeles Herald Examiner*; Margo Osherenko, *California Apparel News*; Eleanor Ringel, *Atlanta Constitution*; Tom Houk, our man in Atlanta; Shelly Wallerstein, our man in D.C.; Joan Luther; Richard Martin, *Nation's Restaurant News*; Nancy J. Adler, *New York Times*; Elizabeth Luft, *The Cleveland Press*; Anne Anable, *The Cleveland Plain Dealer*; Martha Moody and Jack Roarke, *Seasons*; March Schwartz, *Beverly Hills Courier*; Chevy and Ed Foster, *Celebrity Society*; LaVetta Forbes, *Beverly Hills 90212*; Marlo Thomas and the Thomas family; Walter Winchell; Bill Kennedy; Dick Williams; Sidney Skolsky; Cobina Wright; Wanda Henderson Holtzhauser of Les Dames; Mrs. Norman Chandler; Army Archerd, *Variety*; George Christy,

Hollywood Reporter; Seth Baker, Arlene Walsh, Richard Gully, Jack Martin, Gary Amo, Pete LeFevre, *Beverly Hills 213*; Sunny and Warren Adler, *Washington Dossier*; Mike Douglas; Merv Griffin; Carol and Walter Matthau; Billy and Audrey Wilder; Don Krause; Oprah Winfrey; Sally Jesse Raphael; Wesley J. Smith, who encouraged me to write; Brad Lockerman, for all those rounds of golf; Charlie Wessler, Tenner's son, who grew up to be a big producer; Gabrielle Stempel, for reading draft after draft of my manuscript and mobilizing my aching neck; Connie Martinson, who got me with Dorris Halsey, literary agent, who introduced me to Phil Wood and Jo Ann Deck of Ten Speed Press, who assigned project editor Annie Nelson, who chose writer/editor, Brigit L. Binns, who was a joy to work with; Judith Krantz; Jerry Offsay and Sharon Byren of Showtime; Janis Peace, the most giving friend one could have; Solly Biano, for discovering Harry at the Pasadena Playhouse; Jack Warner, who listened to Solly Biano; Irving Lazaar; Freddie de Cordova; Frank Liberman; Dick Carroll; Neil Simon, playwright; Barbara Rush and Warren Cowan; Nancy Jacobs (a stalwart shareholder); Elaine Felderman of Philadelphia; Lilian Prusan of Haven House for battered women and their children, for allowing me to test the waters with a reading of my book; Elizabeth Hansen, for keeping all the photos straight; Michael Jackson, (The British one) of KABC radio, who increased the Hamlet's revenue by 15%; Jon D. Richards, for the wonderful restaurant space allocations, especially the test kitchen; Stan Black, our landlord twice, world traveler, and philanthropist, who taught me that you can still live by the golden rule and that clichés to some are words to live by for others; Jay Weston; Ashley Buck; Lew Siegal; Stan Freberg; Julian Ludwig; Daria and Ed; Bill Kreisel; Kathleen Freeman; Robert Wagner, Natalie Wood, Lily Tomlin, Richard Dreyfus, Rosemary and Robert Stack, Candace Bergen, Blake Edwards, Corky Hale, Tom Hatten, and Jimmy Hulse who are among the first Hamlet babies; all the fantastic Ladies and Gents of the Hamlet; David Wolper; Norman Brokaw; the Lew Wassermans; Susanne Pleshette; Angie Dickenson; Janet de Cordova; Aaron Spelling; Karl Malden; Fred Hayman; Kirk and Anne Douglas; our sons, Adam and David; and finally, the most patient man in the world, Harry Lewis.

CONTENTS

There were no rich relatives, no movie star partners, and we weren't even married at the time. Harry had a dream and I jumped on it, first because I knew I could do it, and it gave me a reason to be close to him. He wanted to open a little restaurant that served good hamburgers. That sounded easy enough. I loved hamburgers. Who doesn't? Nothing stood in my way.

I'm a gambler, but not a gambler who wants to lose. If it took working day and night, that's what it took. I had the energy, the youth, and the will, which propelled me. The $3,500 it took to open our first restaurant came straight from Harry—his life savings from being an actor under contract to Warner Brothers. No movie stars or moguls got together and put up the money, though he tried to interest them…and contrary to rumors, Harry did not marry a girl with independent means. Fortunately, for me, Harry was as hard a worker as I was, and there was none of that "actor" thing with him. Together, we had a lot to learn about the business and about each other. My dream of being a dress designer in Hollywood someday had to be put on hold. Instead, I had to learn to cook. What came into play was: Did our concept have what the public out there needed? Wanted?

Thirty-eight years later and still going strong, we sold out for $33 million. I would say we had what they wanted and we're still together. Turns out I'm still crazy about him.

"THE WORLD AFFORDS NO LAW TO MAKE THEE RICH"

—Romeo and Juliet

I was born in Cleveland in a house full of men. They were my uncles. My mother's brothers. Uncle Carl, Howard, and Myron. My mother, Ruth Laurette, a college dropout, worked all day at a fruit and vegetable stand for $1 a day. I thought she was my big sister or something. I thought "Ann-ma," my grandmother, was my mother. It was the Depression and my grandfather Wolf, whom I called "The Fox," had lost everything except for the big house we lived in and the Packard car, which had once been driven by their uniformed chauffeur. The Fox was in the scrap-iron business, and when his customers started to pay him off with brass candlesticks instead of money, that was it! My Ann-ma became a caterer. It was the only contribution she felt she could make. She sold her lovely baked goods and soups to all their still-wealthy friends. Now they sent their chauffeurs around to pick up her food.

Then I came on the scene. My mother, so young and disillusioned because she had to quit school, pregnant, and work for $1 a day. She and my dad were divorced when I was nine months old. I never saw them as a couple. I couldn't even picture it. He never came to see me, and Ruth Laurette never encouraged it. There was no discussion about him except some disparaging remarks by my mother if he missed paying support money. Five dollars per week. The deadbeat father's law didn't exist then. They were hard times. I was another mouth to feed.

It wasn't until I was six that he finally came around. He took me to Sears & Roebuck for my birthday and bought me a Schwinn two-wheeler. He said he knew how to fix them. He was good with those fine hands, which had once played the violin for the Cleveland Symphony Orchestra. I rode that bike all around the neighborhood, so proudly, for a few weeks. One day, some men carried it away. They said my Dad didn't make the payments.

While Ann-ma catered to make ends meet, I was growing up in her kitchen. All I wanted to do was sketch on the empty front pages in her books. *The message was clear. I wanted to be a dress designer. Not that I could, but the fantasy was very real. Ever since I saw Lana Turner walk down the staircase with a bowl of fruit on her head wrapped in a strapless gown in Ziegfield Follies, I just knew it had to be.*

"To make ends meet" meant nothing to me then. All I knew was that the kitchen smelled so wonderfully delicious all the time. That seemed to even out the quiet hopelessness that permeated the other rooms in the house.

It was hard for everyone, but there was a lot of pride. Ann-ma, who had once played a decent game of bridge with her lady friends in the afternoon, was now selling them her cooking. She was only in her early forties. I remember her black Red Cross, lace up shoes and her swollen ankles. Puffy from standing on her feet so many hours. Having no one to play with, I watched her cook and bake for hours on end. Her workday was never over. And when it was time for the family to have dinner, it was always crisp and white and linen in the formal dining room.

Enter Hattie

She handed my grandmother a note at the door. "Hello, my name is Hattie and I am deaf and dumb. I need a job and will work for room and board, please. Thank You." She was a slender colored* woman who needed a job and would

*the language of the day

trade work for room and board. She was, by her own definition, deaf and dumb, though she could read lips and write notes to make herself understood.

Hattie helped my grandmother do everything: the cooking, the cleaning, the baking. And she raised me.

Hattie was a godsend. With Hattie, Ann-ma was able to expand her cooking to include lemon meringue pies, sweet potato pies, hundreds and hundreds of cheese blintzes, onion soup (which she proudly boasted was made from just a bone), and lobster bisque made from just the empty shells *(the lobster bones)*. The limousines lined up down the street to pick up all this wonderful food.

I spoke to Hattie with no audible voice—only lip movements. She understood me, every word. *She was practically the only one who ever "spoke" in that house.* No matter what she was doing, she'd watch my little face to be sure she didn't miss a word. She was the center of my being.

Every once in awhile, Hattie would disappear wearing my grandmother's Kalinsky fur coat. It turned out she was an alcoholic who went out on little binges from time to time. Whenever my grandmother's Kalinsky fur was missing, we knew Hattie was at one of the neighborhood bars. Ann-ma and I would drive around in the Packard until we found her. She'd sleep it off, have a little hot tea and oatmeal, and everything would be back to normal.

FUN was when she taught me how to use the wringer. I loved watching how it amazingly squeezed out all the water. Being in the basement near that furnace used to scare me, but not with Hattie. I had no one to speak with about anything much, so I lived in silence too, and spoke to Hattie with no voice. *I could not bring myself to raise my hand at school I was so shy. My mind was vital and filled with pictures but I thought I had nothing to say.*

NOT FUN was when I couldn't bring a friend home for lunch. Ann-ma said we simply could not afford it. I told Hattie how I felt about this. A few days later she handed me two sticks of gum. One to share with a friend.

I was learning to play "Edelweiss" on the upright piano when the war broke out with Germany and Japan. I wasn't very good at it but it filled the silence. My handsome Uncle Howard enlisted in the army and fought the Japanese in Bougainville. *A very dangerous place, to me.* His letters were written on grease-stained brown paper bags. It was painful and scary. Ann-ma hung a silk star in the window for Uncle Howard, which was like the yellow ribbons tied around trees today. There were a lot of proud silk stars hanging in the windows on our street and across America.

HAPPY was when *The Lux Hour* aired on the radio on Monday night and *Let's Pretend* aired on Saturdays. *The Hit Parade* was my favorite.

FUN time came when Ann-ma and Hattie took me on a drive down to the steak houses in the flats to collect their empty lobster and shrimp shells. They were so nice about saving them for us. When we got home, we would wrap them in paper bags and a dishtowel and hammer them into little pieces. Then she would boil them in large pots of water until a beautiful fragrant broth would emerge. It was magic! *Sipping a cup of her magic was the most wonderful reward for me. Now I wish I had been helping her—little did I know that someday I would have to learn to cook in a very big way!*

"For Now, I Stand as One upon a Rock"

—Titus Andronicus

I didn't know my mother was getting married. I didn't even know she was seeing anyone until she introduced this man, John J. Shear, as my new daddy. I had no particular feelings at the time about this new set of events until she told me I was going to live with them and that I was leaving Ann-ma's house. *Leaving Hattie and going to live in an apartment with my new stepfather. A person I didn't know.*

Mother told me to tell my Ann-ma that I was leaving her. The feelings came hard when I had to do this. Would she feel rejected? Would she feel relief? It was my first lesson in diplomacy and kindness. I was only ten. Today a ten-year-old can grapple with that sort of thing, but then, divorce was like a scourge. To be yanked out of your home was a stupefying experience. Forcing a child to choose between parent figures is a terrible thing. Ann-ma had raised me. *And Hattie. I was going to leave them!* In her own gentle and mannered way, Ann-ma said simply, "It's alright, dear, you must come and visit." *My heart ached.*

They put my bedroom in the dining room. There was no door *and no privacy.*

My mother bought me a pair of brown ice skates when I was thirteen. I wished they had been white, not brown, but, since I didn't know how to figure-skate anyway, it didn't matter. Brown, I thought, looked more athletic, so instead of spinning and twirling, I raced. Round and round, faster and faster. What joy!

The boys started to take note. A very pink and white girl I saw on the ice, named Lois Peltz, became a friend. One day she asked if I would like to join her sorority. I didn't know what all that was about, but I said yes. She would arrange for me to meet her sorority sisters.

They all lived in Shaker Heights, the wealthiest suburb in Cleveland. I lived on Parkwood Drive in "The City," *on the wrong side of the tracks.* Lois lived in a brick mansion up on a hill. I lived in an apartment house.

I took a long bus ride to meet her friends. They all liked me, she said, and they wanted me to pledge. They gave me a pledge pin, which I wore proudly on my sweater. But on the rink, Lois told me there was one problem: I had to live in the Heights or in Shaker to become a member. Did I have a relative who would allow me to use their address?

I immediately thought of my Aunt Riv, who was married to a wealthy attorney and lived in University Heights. My mother asked her for me, and she agreed. Lois was thrilled and said it would be our secret. One of the boys at the rink, Sandy Miller, was seemingly very interested in me. *He looked like Peter Lawford. I had such a crush on him. My first. He was a rich kid who lived in University Heights. When he found out I lived in "The City" his attention waned. I was heartbroken. But when Lois told him that her sorority was pledging me, the little flicker was on again.*

Those days were a kind of heaven I had never known. But I was living a lie, pretending. There was no way I could keep up with those girls, but I didn't think about it. I thought of Sandy and the joy I felt on the ice, floating on brown skates.

After a few months of this, the time had come: the meeting to decide which of the girls would be admitted to the sorority. Pledge time was over. I took the long bus ride to a beautiful home high up on a grassy hill.

All the boys from the fraternities were outside waiting, including Sandy. I passed them and went inside. Lois and the girls were all there. When it came to my turn, the president announced angrily that the girls had discovered that I did not live on Edgerton Road at all. This kind of deception was a waste of their time.

They tore my pledge pin off my sweater and de-pledged me.

I had to walk past all the boys again, ashamed, and take the long bus ride home. I didn't go ice-skating any more and I never saw Lois or Sandy again.

"To Me, Fair Friend, You Can Never Be Old"

—Sonnet 104

Then I met Tenner. Ruth Tenner.

"Sit there and count your fingers, little girl blue" (a strain I hear during particularly sad times).

She brought joy into my life.

We had so much in common. She lived in "The City." She was an only child just like me. She loved clothes. Angora sweaters and penny loafers. Her mother, Sally, was also divorced.

Sally Tenner could have been a silent screen star. She dressed like one. Stilettos, a Silver Fox jacket, lots of lipstick, and a gardenia in her hair.

We fantasized together about her mother and my father getting married, so we could be sisters. *I knew where my father lived. On Olivett Avenue. Hattie had walked me by once, to show me.* Ruth and I planned an adventure. We would go to my dad's house and tell him about Sally. One day we got up the nerve and did it. We boldly walked up on the porch and rang the bell—he was home. The minute he came to the door, we babbled on about him meeting Sally, Ruth's mom. He had a very jolly nature, and agreed to meet her. Sam and Sally went out on a date, but it didn't take. *We were heartbroken.*

I knew I couldn't live in my dear mother's home anymore. It was too hard for her. Her new husband, JJ, had four of his own children, and they were all at an orphanage. Who was I to have the honored choice of living at home with my mother and *their* father? Early on, I knew it couldn't be. *Hattie must have known I'd need my own father one day. That's why she had walked me past his house on Olivett when I was very little.*

I Hitchhiked My Way to California. Age 14.

My dad and I made a secret plan. He would drive across country and I would hitchhike, (more or less). I would be safe with the truckers, and he would be right behind them. Daddy's sister Frances worked in a truck dispatch office and she arranged it all. World War II was on.

The plan was that only my new grandmother (Daddy's mother) and his sister would know where we were. They would keep it from my mother.

Daddy and I would have a new life together and start over. We were to meet at a particular truck stop in San Bernadino. Had I gone with him and my mother found us, the authorities would have taken Daddy to jail and I would have had to return to Cleveland.

The truckers were wonderful. They knew they were breaking the law, but they took the chance. Carrying a minor over state lines had its consequences. They hid me, fed me, traded me from one truck to another, and mostly they were kind. One young one bought me a ten cent ring and asked to marry me. I told him he'd have to ask my Daddy's permission at the next stop. But he never got the chance. I got away from his truck and immediately on to another that rolled right on schedule into California. Daddy was watching my every move.

Our timing worked out perfectly. There was my Dad right there among the onions and the leeks, just as we'd talked about. He had come across Route 66. Now my Daddy could be a musician at a big studio and I might even become a movie star!

"Then Westward Ho!"

—Twelfth Night

It was D-day, June 6th, 1944 when we met in Los Angeles to begin our new life. Our very first stop in L.A. had to be the Musicians' Union, so he could sign up and wait out his six months. Meanwhile he would work in the Vallejo defense plants. That way, he'd be able to get gas ration coupons and earn a living while he waited hopefully for a position with a studio orchestra.

A man with my dad's credentials—it had to be a shoo-in.

My dad had been the youngest violinist in the Cleveland Symphony Orchestra, under the direction of Nikolai Sokoloff. (Born in Kiev, he was the first conductor of the orchestra, prior to Maestro George Szell, from 1918 to 1933.) Dad was only sixteen, but he played so well that they made him a member of this great orchestra. When my mother married him, she was able to sit in the front row and watch this great *assembly of men playing under all these great conductors. Dad was earning $150 a week—a lot of money in 1929. When my parents divorced, mother claimed that Dad had blackened her eye, and that was that. I understand my grandfather, The Fox, went after him. Later, he began drinking from loneliness, and was thrown out of the orchestra. His income was gone, his drinking was up, and all he could do was teach violin to the neighborhood kids, who didn't have two dimes to rub together.*

Standing at the Musicians' Union desk, Dad filled out the union papers, when a small thin woman yelled, "Sam? Sam, is that you?"

"Anna?" They hugged and hugged. Then Dad introduced me. Anna was a piano teacher whom he knew from Cleveland. They grew up together as children, and now she was living out here in Hollywood, because her brother, Albert Saks, was a famous studio musician and had his own orchestra! It was too good to be true. Dad told her about our plans to make a new life and asked if she knew where I might be able to live while he spent most of the week working in Vallejo. She immediately offered me the spare bed in her apartment. I was with Anna every day. We waited for Daddy to come down from Vallejo on the weekends. *This was my new life. I counted the days on the calendar.*

We were a very happy threesome. Then one day, Daddy took me aside and told me that he and Anna were going to be married. I was thrilled! He went on to explain that since she had always loved him, all of her life, she would like not to be reminded that Dad had ever been married before. "When I married your mother, it broke her heart. She does not want you to be at the actual wedding. She does not want to be reminded that I already have a daughter. Not on her wedding day." She wanted to live out her fantasy and pretend that she was his first marriage.

"My beautiful little Marilyn, you know I love you." My daddy said to me so sweetly. "You understand, don't you?" (A rhetorical question.)

I could understand, for him. *I was quiet. Empty.*

He promised we would be together in just a little while, after they were married, especially when his new brother-in-law, Albert Saks, got him settled into a studio orchestra. (He never did.)

On his wedding day, Dad found a room for me. It was on South Harvard in Hollywood. 849 South Harvard. Grace, a registered nurse, owned the house and rented all the bedrooms out to single actresses. I was almost fifteen, and I wasn't an actress. *Not yet.* I had some serious liabilities: I was shy and soft-spoken. Alone now, and surrounded by beautiful young actresses, I soaked up everything they could teach me. Like how to make "Ann Sheridan lips" and to get work as an extra. An extra with a few good wardrobe pieces might get a speaking part. *But where would this money come from?* Daddy would not be able to help me financially—he had a new wife.

I knew I had to make a plan. It was survival time. I went to work as a carhop and saved my money. I found Nancy's, a dress shop on Hollywood Blvd., and there I bought my "Hollywood clothes": a beautiful peplum dress, black on the bottom and fuchsia on top; and a Joan Crawford pantsuit in royal blue, with big padded shoulders. Two weeks later, after making the rounds, I was actually hired for an ice-skating role in *Margie* at 20th Century Fox. Jeanne Crain was the star. I found my glow, but then my mother found me. *It was back to Cleveland…*

"Lowliness Is Young Ambition's Ladder"

—Julius Caesar

Attending Glenville High School in my sophomore year was like walking through some kind of haze. Nothing was fun. Thank goodness for Tenner. Once in awhile, she and I would double-date and I would wear my Hollywood clothes—they made me look older. One day, I read in the newspaper that the Higbee Company was looking for Junior Miss Models. *Once I got that into my head, it was all I could think about.* Very quietly, I applied for the job. Threw my shoulders back, walked like Jeannie Crain, and got it!

I began to feel some sense of worth. I was wearing beautiful clothes, and moved so gracefully in them. I watched the professional models glide and turn, and emulated the same movements. Very much like a child dances. *I felt free.*

Nina Ricci, a famous Parisian couturier, was coming to Cleveland to stage her first fashion show in America. She was using all the fabrics that had been hoarded through the war years—the show was the big news of the day—*and I was in it! Not only in the show, but chosen to be the bride, the most coveted part.*

I invited my mother and Tenner to the Statler Hotel to see me. Walking down the runway was like an out-of-body experience. My mother was truly stunned and very proud. *I had never seen that particular emotion from her before.* There was a man in the audience who sent his card backstage to me: Dr. LoPreste. He owned a modeling school called The House of Charm, and he wanted me to teach a class for Junior Miss Models. He spoke with my mother, and a contract was drawn. I earned $100 a week for teaching a two-hour class, three nights a week, after school. *No one caught on that I had no formal training.* I was able to give my mother some money every week, which felt very good.

There I was, teaching all these little junior high school girls, and some older women too. Some of them clearly were not model material. I asked the receptionist, Elaine, how the doctor could take money from some of these unqualified model hopefuls? She shrugged her shoulders and said, "Business." Many of the girls complained to the Better Business Bureau, when they got no job placement, just as I had expected. The newspapers were not kind. The exposé was killing. But the girls liked me.

Dr. LoPreste asked if I would like to buy his business. *He was on the run.* Elaine and I concurred that there was no business to buy—we would just start our own by asking the students to continue on with us. They all signed up. *Now I had my own business. I was sixteen. The only problem: the students could not know how young I was, and they could not know that I was still in school. Elaine kept my secret.*

Every day, I would come home from school, put on a grown-up hat, and take the long streetcar ride down to my new offices at 1290 Euclid Avenue in the Flatiron Building. Quickly, I added a finishing school program. That way we could offer diction, elocution, poise, walking, posture, and ballet, along with makeup, hair, and diet. This appealed to a wide range of women, not just the modeling hopefuls. *I don't know where it came from, but there I was writing all the lessons I would preach to women older than myself, as if I had been doing it for years. It was almost like an angel's hand was moving mine.*

I didn't just train the models, I got them jobs. I couldn't take their money unless I could give it back in some way. *It wasn't in my nature.* I stumped the sidewalks, department stores, conventions. It was a hard sell, but in the process I learned about marketing. Marketing 101.

It was during this period that I met Herb Kline, the director from Hollywood. He was in Cleveland making a film called *The Kid from Cleveland,* starring George Brent, Rusty Tamblyn, and Lynn Bari. Mister Kline needed a few beautiful extras to appear in the film, and was told to call me. He was a very fatherly, soft-spoken man with kind, pale green eyes, slightly slanted. *A feature, he told me, that only happened if your ancestors were raped by the Philistines.* I found him profoundly interesting, though of course he was too old for me. He said to call him if I ever got to Hollywood and he would introduce me to a few people. I kept his number.

"My Salad Days, When I Was Green in Judgment"

—Antony and Cleopatra

Tenner graduated from high school and married an army captain. He was stationed in Los Angeles, so off she went to her new life. *This was a blow. Now there was no one.*

Cleveland paled again, but now I was older. One year later, I too followed my dream and went to Hollywood. I sold the modeling agency to Elaine, and set out to begin my next career: to become a dress designer.

The director, Herb Kline, was quite surprised when I phoned to tell him I was coming to Hollywood. He was caught off guard, thinking that I expected something of him. *A typical reaction among the Hollywood crowd. "Everyone always wants something."* He sounded rather disinterested about the whole thing.

Tenner and her husband, Dick, made a place for me in their little valley home on Whitsett. I drove Laurel Canyon, all 164 curves of it, back and forth each day to visit Herb. To visit his home was to meet some very interesting, well-known writers, like Aben Kandell, who wrote the wonderful film *City for Conquest*. Kandell's wife had written *Dear Ruth*, a Broadway hit. *The first time I was there she invited me to go home with her husband "because he liked young pretty things." What do you say? "Thanks, but…"?*

They all knew Hemingway and Faulkner personally. I was in awe of these people. They had read so much—Kafka, Shaw, Dostoyevsky. Everything they talked about ended in "esque." As in, Kafka-esque. Or the other term: "right out of." ("Right out of George Bernard Shaw" or "Right out of Dostoyevsky.") I had read none of these books. They spoke in such feeling terms, which I had never heard before or explored. The words *empathy*, *sensitivity*, and *sensibility* were played over and over. It was a revelation. *Ethos* and *pathos*. That they were full of bullshit didn't matter. They would gather to put each other on.

Jim Nablo, with one published book to his credit, would get lachrymose at not having gone to Spain during the war. The guys would holler out, "Let's hear it for the unseen warrior!" Everyone would howl! *So terribly Hollywood it was.*

Jim was a charmer. His wife was this waif-like presence from the South, but tough as nails. Following one of her whining Southern opines, the writer Arthur Ross threw out this: "Come on, no more of that Belle shit!"

All this amusing dialogue was flying around constantly. *Some of it over my head.* Herb romanticized everything: His time in Spain during the war, when he played war correspondent and photographer, emulating Ernie Pyle and quoting Hemingway.

Herb's compulsion to pepper his conversations with sex so exasperated Arthur Ross, that one night, after Herb's endless sexual essay, he waited to deliver the punch:

"Herb, your fly is open! You're gonna catch a death of a cold in your penis."

'Penis?!' Who used this word? This is a word I had never heard spoken before, much less thought about. (Long before Howard Stern.)

Herb retorted, "You better be nice to me, Arthur, because someday, you're going to be very rich, and rich people don't have many friends."

There was one guy who always "knew" every author they were discussing. The gang decided they had to get him. So Arthur, Jim, and lyricist Paul Francis Webster ("I've Got It Bad and That Ain't Good") made up a whole new school of authors, having to do with a (supposedly) new existentialist movement. They laid it on really thick, and they caught him good. Because, surprise, surprise, he knew all about that new movement, too.

Their satirical repartee sometimes bordered on the Sturm und Drang: No one knew where reality began or ended, especially me, and even if you changed the subject, the drone went on and on. But the level of self-deprecating humor was infectious.

I was invited, often, to sit on the floor and listen. I was also expected to wash the dishes and straighten up the mess created at these gatherings. *I was now their maid, picking up after them, but I didn't mind.* I thought Herb would be able to introduce me to the right people, so that I could show my sketches and hope for an apprenticeship. In some ways I was world weary, but still willing to work and learn for however long it took. I wanted to be someone who mattered. I wanted to glow.

One Hollywood night Herb took me to the Players' Ring Theater, where I met the actor Harry Lewis. And that's where the story begins.

"Broil the Burger, I Pray You…"

HARRY, IN CHEF'S HAT, TAKES
ORDERS FROM LEX BARKER
(A FAVORITE TARZAN) AND ARLENE
DAHL (LORENZO LAMAS' MOM).

PART ONE

Are You Sure You Can Cook?

The Players' Ring Theater was a theater in the round, and this was new for me. They were doing Elmer Rice's *Street Scene*, and the naughty milkman was absolutely gorgeous! His name was Harry Lewis.

Because the theater was round, I could see him and he, I was certain, could see me. There I sat in my (one and only) little black dress, string of pearls (not real), opera pumps, and little white kid gloves.

Luckily, Herb knew Harry and said he would take me backstage after the play. It was "Hello, you were great," and that was that. *I felt very shy again, the way you feel around actors…*

I went back by myself three nights in a row. All I could think about was this actor Harry Lewis. I was smitten. On the third night I made my way backstage with all the other fans, just as I had twice before, and waited. But this time, Harry noticed me.

"Hello." he said. "You've been back to see the show…"

I nodded and smiled.

"How does one reach you?"

I answered in a most affected, low "Lauren Bacall" tone, a tone I didn't even know was inside me: "One places their finger in the dial…." And I gave him my number.

This is the Harry I met at the Players' Ring Theater.

top Harry with Academy Award winner Claire Trevor, in *Key Largo*.
middle With Edward G. Robinson.
bottom With Bogart.

On our first date, we traded stories. Harry told me he had been under contract to Warner Brothers, and they had just dropped his option after seven years and almost forty movies. He'd saved his money and was now scraping by, waiting for the next break.

His biggest role had been in *Key Largo*, directed by John Huston and starring Humphrey Bogart, Lauren Bacall, Edward G. Robinson, and Claire Trevor. (Claire Trevor won the Academy Award for her incredible portrayal of Robinson's drunken girlfriend.) Harry played Edward G. Robinson's handsome young, gun-toting bodyguard. He was in almost every scene and he was good! (Or rather, he was good at being a bad guy.)

I had never known an actor before. Not even an out-of-work actor.

"What happens now?" I asked. "Is there life after Warner Brothers?"

"I've always wanted to open a little restaurant, a little place where agents, actors, writers, and directors could hang out. Nothing fancy—just a little place with good hamburgers. Something I could work at myself in between acting jobs."

I wondered if he really meant it, or if it was just a dream. I knew about dreams. Mine was that one day I'd meet my idols: Walter Plunkett (who designed all those dreamy Marlene Dietrich outfits) and Edith Head, the doyenne of Paramount's costume department. And one day my biggest dream would come true. I would be a dress designer, too.

I felt a rush of excitement. I wanted his dream to be real and I wanted to help him do it. I told him so. *Too fast. This was still our first date.*

After I swore I'd never tell a soul, he revealed the name of his dream restaurant.

"Hamburger Hamlet," he whispered.

"What does that mean?" I asked.

"Hamlet," he said. "Every actor wants to play Hamlet! It's every actor's apogee."

"What's an apogee?" I asked.

He kissed me. Probably to shut me up.

That night, on our very first date, we went out looking for a location. *This was an interesting first date.* Of course, we didn't find anything. We hadn't even a clue of what we were looking for. It was a dance. A dance first-daters do sometimes to create their time together. That night, I couldn't sleep. All I could think of was Harry and the menu, so I sat up half the night writing it.

The next morning, I called him.

"I want to read you the menu." I was headlong in a crush and had to have a reason to call him. He seemed tentative. I guess he wasn't expecting all this activity, to put it mildly.

I wrote that menu the same way I'd learned to write the narration for the fashion shows we used to do back in Cleveland. But this time, it was about hamburgers.

How I remembered the smell of those hamburgers, as I stood in front of the White Castle in Cleveland. I remembered wishing I had forty cents for a bagful. I remembered Mawby's up on Cedar Road, when I transferred buses to get to Shaker Heights. Those wonderful onions piled so high on the grill, all pink from paprika. You could smell their luscious aroma every time the door opened and closed.

I could tell he didn't know what to make of me. He was baffled. I was moving too fast. He'd shared a fantasy with me, but perhaps that was all it was. Did he call? Yes, now and then, just to touch base. Had I invaded his dream?

Herb had introduced me to film producer Murray Lippert, who owned his own studio. I was ambitious, and he thought I might get a spot as an apprentice in the design department (this did not happen). One day Mr. Lippert phoned to ask if I would accompany him to temple in Boyle Heights for Yom Kippur, where he was due to meet his mother.

This seemed a far cry from the design department.

I wore my (one and only) little black dress, string of pearls (not real), and white kid gloves. The limousine picked me up and as we drove down Sunset Boulevard, I noticed a "For Rent" sign. At the corner of Hilldale and Sunset, right on the Sunset strip.

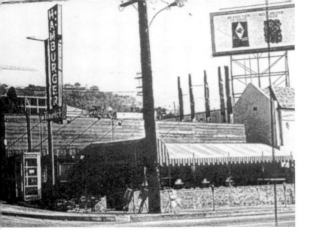

I felt my nose wiggle. In later years, my nose would select all our new locations. It was quite a marketing tool.

My heart raced as I jotted down the number. We got to the temple and I could hardly sit still—I had to get to a telephone. The producer assured me that nothing was open on this important high holiday. I excused myself and ran down the street to find—*please dear God*—a phone.

A little Mexican market was open and had a pay phone! I was so excited I could hardly speak. When Harry answered, I urged him to call the number. He said he would.

Three or four hours later, I was home. The phone rang. "(Cough, cough, cough) I'm here with the landlord." It was Harry.

"Yes!"

"He wants two hundred and fifty dollars a month…." His voice sounded weird.

"Yes!"

"Two hundred and fifty dollars a month! That times twelve…!!??" He sounded worse.

"That's great," I yelled through the phone. "Give it to him!"

"I'll call you back," he said.

I must mention that every time Harry gets nervous, he makes little coughing sounds. Each one of those phone calls started with little coughing sounds. He still does this.

The phone rang! "(Cough, cough, cough) He wants me to sign a lease for ten years!!!!!"

"Sign it!" I screamed. He hung up.

The phone rang.

"(Cough, cough, cough) okay, he wants me to sign a lease for five years!!!"

"Take it! Take it!" I yelled. I was very excited.

"Take it?" he asked, "A five-year lease???" He was half whispering now.

"Yes! Yes! Can you buy the property?" I asked.

He hung up on me.

The phone rang.

"(Cough, cough) I just signed the lease." There was a pause. "Marilyn…"

Pause.

"ARE YOU SURE YOU CAN COOK?"

MUCH ADO ABOUT A MENU

We hadn't even "been" together and he was expecting me to cook? *He signed a lease because he thought I could cook.* The answer was "No," I couldn't cook—cook what? What was I going to do? What could I do? I couldn't tell Harry. *He signed a lease.*

"Tenner, what'll I do?" I anguished.

"Buy a cookbook." she offered.

I bought *The Brown Derby Cookbook* because it had cheese blintzes in it.

My grandmother used to pile those crêpes up to the ceiling, cooking all day "to make ends meet," she always said. She'd take those crêpes and wrap them up into little bundles, some around jelly and some around a white, slightly tart cream. Those were the cheese blintzes. I had not one of my grandmother's recipes, but the appearance and the aroma of her food was indelibly etched in my mind.

A Brown Derby Cookbook Recipe

CHEESE BLINTZES, Serves 6

3¾ 2 eggs
⁴⁄₄₆ 1 cup milk
8½ ½ tsp. salt
Little orange and lemon peel finely grated
8½ c ½ cup flour
3 tsp. butter

1½ cups cottage cheese
1 cup sour cream
½ tsp. ginger
1 tsp. vanilla
2 tsp. sugar
1 cup currant or strawberry jelly

To prepare batter: Beat eggs. Add milk, salt, and peel. Pour into the flour slowly, stirring vigorously to obtain a smooth, thin batter. Pour 2 tbs. of the batter into a 7-in. frying pan that has been very slightly buttered, spreading thin over the entire bottom of the pan. When cooked, the edges will shrink away from the side of the pan. Remove the pancake and invert on cloth or paper that has been sprinkled with powdered sugar. Allow to cool.

FILLING: Blend cottage cheese, one half of sour cream, ginger, vanilla, and sugar. Put 2 tbs. of filling in the center of each of the pancakes. Roll like a jelly roll and place in a shallow pan. When all of the cakes have been filled, place a dab of butter on top of each and put under broiler (or in oven at 350°) until heated through. Serve, topped with balance of sour cream and jelly.

48

The cookbook could not be used as it was—recipes for six would never make it. How many customers would order cheese blintzes? Certainly more than six, but probably less than twenty? It was all guesswork. In the margins of the pages, I pondered. I multiplied eggs times five and flour times five and milk times five, which would give us around thirty orders. *No that's way too much.*

Okay, then two and a half times, which would give us around fifteen orders…and that may be way too much. How can you possibly know?

What a shame I didn't know I would need grandmother's recipes some day.

Like her lobster bisque. This was absolutely the most wonderful thing you could ever eat. *A bowl of magic.* I remembered the flavor of the bisque, but I didn't know how to make it. I racked my mind until I saw some images, of some of the ingredients she might have used.

Those images were so real. Driving in the Packard down to the waterfront, where the lobster restaurants would save the empty lobster shells for my Ann-ma. Going home in that sweet lobster-smelling car. Oh yes, I remember we drove to the butcher shop to pick up soup bones for her onion soup. My mind was racing. Yes! We had to have her onion soup, too!

I had to think about the hamburgers. There were so many dressings and ideas to draw from. We could have one with Russian dressing and real caviar. We could do one with barbecue sauce. We could do one with just plain catsup, or we could do one with chili, chopped onions, and grated cheese. What if an actress was on a diet? I thought we could do one on a plate with no bun and add sauerkraut (128 calories). I had worked with those skinny models in the fashion shows, and that's the way they ate. Then, the most delicious idea popped into my brain: a hamburger topped with melted cheese, bacon, and Russian dressing! I couldn't wait to try it. It sounded so good. That had to be a killer, I thought. (Not only was it the most popular hamburger on the menu, but it probably had enough cholesterol to do the job!)

It was like designing clothes—I just sensed what would go well together, and it worked.

I had heard Löwenbraü beer pronounced "Ler-ven-brau" at Hazan's Market and I thought it sounded swell because you had to know how to pronounce it. I put it on the menu.

Ice cream from Wil Wright's sounded swell, too. And Cherries Jubilee, which I once tasted at the Statler Hotel while modeling in the Nina Ricci fashion show. Never was there such a menu in such a little place!

Harry said Wil Wright would certainly not go for us putting his ice cream on our menu. Not only was it expensive, but it was exclusively sold in Wil Wright's ice cream shops. "Well, let's see if he will," I said, determined.

I called Mr. Wright and he came over to the empty shell we had just leased on the Sunset Strip. *That he even came over was remarkable to me.*

"Everything starts with an idea and an empty space, or an empty canvas, like the arts," I told him. I sat him on an orange crate and asked him to visualize our dream. "This wall will be hunter green and that wall will be copper…." He loved sitting on that orange crate and sharing our dream. He could see it right along with me. We got his ice cream, including the use of his little painted logo: An angel, with a halo proclaiming, "It's Heavenly!" It was like a personal endorsement from Mr. Wil Wright himself. He was an ice cream celebrity! (There were no food celebrities then.) I was told that rich kids asked to have their allowances increased so they could go to Wil Wright's. Now they could get his ice cream at our little Hamlet.

His ice cream was the richest in the world: 32% butterfat (so fatty, it actually stuck to the roof of your mouth, which was considered good at the time). It was also the highest-priced…and worth every single penny!

I felt our angel had arrived, even if it was an ice cream angel. Harry was overwhelmed with my expensive notions.

It was not easy opening a restaurant. There was a lot to learn. Harry was still acting and going for auditions while we built the little place. I took a job as a counter waitress at Simon's All-Night Drive-In. It was a perfect place to learn what not to do. We kept the name secret until the day we opened. I think I told one of the waitresses on my shift at Simon's. She gave me a funny look….

Harry picked me up every morning at six o'clock and I gave him all my tips from the night before, about fifteen dollars. He was saving them for me, *which was my own idea. After all, he was putting up $3,500 of his life's earnings, so it seemed like the right thing to do. It was a small, innocent gesture, but I felt that it counted.*

The "Hamlet" took shape. It was very warm and inviting, like a rec room in an Eastern home. All knotty pine and maple trim. The bar-high counter was the centerpiece that wrapped around the copper-hooded fireplace/barbecue. Ten tall, backless bar stools sat in front of the bar. *The stools soon become favorites with every celebrity you can imagine.* In the adjoining little pine-paneled dining room were six redwood tables and benches from Sears & Roebuck (the layaway plan), which seated a total of twenty-four.

I studied nutrition, studied cookbooks. I practiced and practiced. Read cookbooks every night like detective novels (the only thing wrong with this method is that it makes you hungry late at night). I learned to imagine the tastes,

'I tried to borrow money from all my friends in the motion picture business. Jack Warner, Humphrey Bogart, Cesar Romero, Gig Young. I tried to borrow $5,000, $3,000, $1,000. I said, "How about $500?" Nobody would give us a cent,' says Harry, noting that construction was underway and they still showed a negative cash flow. Marilyn convinced him to invest his last $3,500. 'She said to me, "You'll never be sorry," so I put the $3,500 into the business and I've never been sorry.'
— *Fortune* magazine

"A mind stretched by new
ideas never does go back
to its original size.
And neither does your waistline."
—*Anonymous*

as if I was eating. Every recipe was made over and over until it was perfect. I was learning, and Harry was so patient. He would eat the practice food over and over until I got it right, then we would invite friends to dinner and serve it up proudly. He was, of course, to act as if he had never tasted it before. He was the actor here, and he played his role well.

I wanted to take "fancy" foods down a peg. It was an interesting juxtaposition.

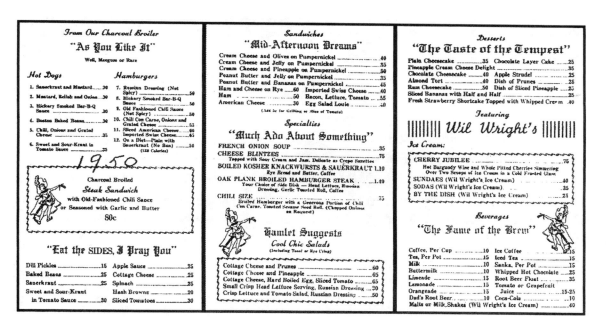

When people are all suited up in black tie, I found that most of them actually prefer eating comfort foods, instead of the usual "things under glass" or bland veal chops. This was certainly a part of the success of the Hamlets. Who would expect lobster bisque, Cherries Jubilee, and French onion soup brought down to the level where one could comfortably dine in blue jeans, no tie, or black tie, sitting next to a favorite movie star and at half the price? This can be a lot of fun.

It was new. Revolutionary in 1950, but it sure got everyone's attention. One could say it was risky. That too.

LOBSTER BISQUE

SERVES 6

THIS CAN LOOK VERY OVERWHELMING—
TAKE TWO DAYS AND IT WILL GO EASILY.

Is it worth it? Yes. There will be lots of cleanup to do; good if you have a helper. My grandmother made and sold this soup for her wealthy patrons every day during the Depression years, without lobster meat—with the shells only. This is totally amazing to me. It amazes me that I was there, a tiny girl, to watch her hammer the shells to a pulp in a paper bag and boil them until the sweet fragrance permeated my senses. It was obviously important to me, too, because it became a crucial part of our first business success. Having lobster bisque in a little hamburger joint resonated across America. Yes, one little place and one wonderful soup did all that. Harry (who was an actor, certainly not a cook) spent hours making this magical broth every night in the back of our home so that no one would ever have the recipe. Now you do.

Fortunately, there is a sweetness about the aroma or I would have left him long ago. My grandmother is responsible for the notion to do such an illustrious soup, although hers was so spare, made from the lobster shells only. This one doesn't dare to be so spare, yet it does have some savings to it. One live lobster and lots of shrimp work out just fine.

THE FIRST DAY: COOKING THE LOBSTER

❧ IN A WIDE POT WITH A LID, BRING TO RAPID BOIL:

    8 CUPS WATER

    2 TEASPOONS KOSHER SALT

❧ POP INTO THE WATER HEAD FIRST:

1 1/2 POUND LIVE MAINE LOBSTER (CUT BANDS OFF THE CLAWS FIRST)

꙳ COVER AND SET THE TIMER FOR 11 MINUTES, NO MORE.

꙳ SET THE LOBSTER ASIDE ON A RIDGED PAN TO COLLECT ANY JUICES FOR THE LOBSTER BROTH WE WILL DO NEXT. REMOVE AND REFRIGERATE THE LOBSTER TAIL MEAT, AND RESERVE FOR THE FINAL GARNISH.

If you're smart, you will twist off the claws and eat the warm meat yourself right now.

MAKING THE LOBSTER BROTH

꙳ STRAIN THE WATER YOU USED FOR COOKING THE LOBSTER INTO A LARGE DUTCH OVEN. THERE SHOULD BE 6 CUPS.

꙳ PEEL, DEVEIN, AND SAVE ALL THE SHELLS OF:

1 POUND MEDIUM SHRIMP

RESERVE THE SHRIMPS.

꙳ THROW THE EMPTY SHRIMP SHELLS INTO THE LOBSTER WATER WITH:

12 WHITE PEPPERCORNS

FEW SPRIGS OF FRESH THYME

THE EMPTY LOBSTER SHELL

꙳ BRING TO A BOIL. IMMEDIATELY TURN DOWN THE HEAT AND SIMMER GENTLY, COVERED, FOR 30 MINUTES. *Covered because we don't want it to reduce.*

꙳ STRAIN THE LOBSTER STOCK THROUGH A COLANDER LINED WITH A DOUBLE THICKNESS OF CHEESECLOTH INTO A LARGE BOWL OR ANOTHER POT. SET ASIDE. DISCARD THE LOBSTER AND SHRIMP SHELLS. WIPE OUT THE DUTCH OVEN WITH A PAPER TOWEL.

❦ ADD TO THE CLEAN DUTCH OVEN, OVER MEDIUM HEAT:

2 TABLESPOONS SWEET BUTTER

❦ SAUTÉ FOR 4 MINUTES OVER MEDIUM HEAT, TURNING,

UNTIL PINK:

THE RESERVED RAW SHRIMP

SET ASIDE IN A BOWL.

You will notice the brown "fond" from the shrimp will be on the bottom of the pot. Do not scrape it away, it is full of good flavors. Just leave it be for now.

❦ THIS IS WHERE YOU CAN STOP AND REFRIGERATE EVERYTHING

UNTIL TOMORROW, IF YOU WANT. OR WE CAN CONTINUE.

❦ USING THE SAME POT OVER MEDIUM-LOW HEAT, THROW IN:

1 TABLESPOON SWEET BUTTER

❦ AND THEN:

1 MEDIUM YELLOW ONION, DICED

$^1/_2$ CUP SLICED CARROTS

$^1/_2$ CUP SLICED CELERY

A FEW MORE SPRIGS OF FRESH THYME

1 $^1/_2$ TEASPOONS GRATED FRESH LEMON PEEL (BEING CAREFUL

NOT TO INCLUDE THE BITTER WHITE PITH UNDER THE

LEMON-COLORED RIND)

❦ MIX AROUND WITH WOODEN SPOON FOR ABOUT 8 MINUTES,

UNTIL TENDER.

❦ ADD TO THE PAN:

1 CUP DRY WHITE WINE

$^1/_2$ CUP DRY SHERRY

4 TABLESPOONS TOMATO PASTE (I LIKE THE REFRIGERATED

TUBES, WHICH ARE VERY CONVENIENT AND THERE IS NO WASTE.)

☙ BRING TO A BOIL FOR ABOUT 2 MINUTES TO BURN OFF THE
ALCOHOL.

☙ NOW IS THE TIME TO SCRAPE THE BROWN "FOND" FROM THE
BOTTOM WITH A WOODEN SPOON AND MIX ALL ITS GOODNESS
INTO THE LOVELY LIQUID THAT WILL EMERGE.

☙ ADD TO THE DUTCH OVEN:

ALL OF THE RESERVED LOBSTER AND SHRIMP STOCK

I CUP HEAVY CREAM

I CUP LOW-FAT, LOW-SODIUM CHICKEN BROTH

6 TABLESPOONS RAW LONG-GRAIN WHITE RICE

☙ COVER THE POT AND SIMMER UNTIL THE RICE IS TENDER,
ABOUT 20 MINUTES.

☙ BRING BACK THE LITTLE SHRIMP AND THE VEGETABLE-WINE
MIXTURE, AND OFF WE WILL GO TO THE BLENDER.

☙ THIS IS THE TEDIOUS PART. IT TAKES A LITTLE TIME AND
MUSCLE. IF YOU HAVE A FRIEND THAT YOU CAN BRIBE WITH A
LOBSTER CLAW, YOU CAN TAKE TURNS.

☙ COMBINE SOME OF THE LOBSTER-RICE BROTH WITH A LITTLE
SHRIMP, AND SOME OF THE WINE-BRAISED VEGETABLES,
FILLING THE BLENDER JAR ONLY HALFWAY. DO SEVERAL
SMALL BATCHES AND EMPTY EACH BATCH INTO A FINE-MESHED
STRAINER SET OVER A FRESH CLEAN POT. USING A BIG RUBBER
SPATULA, PUSH, PUSH, PUSH, UNTIL YOU HAVE THE CLEAR
CORAL PINK BROTH SEPARATED FROM THE DRY PULP.

☙ ADD TO THE LOBSTER BROTH:

$^1/_4$ TEASPOON CAYENNE PEPPER

I TEASPOON SALT, OR TO TASTE

☙ CREATE A DOUBLE BOILER, IF YOU DON'T HAVE ONE, BY

PLACING A SMALLER PAN OVER A LARGER PAN FILLED WITH
SIMMERING WATER. (THIS IS IMPORTANT, AS CREAMED
SOUPS HAVE A TENDENCY TO SCORCH EASILY.)

AT POINT OF SERVICE, YOU WILL NEED

TOASTED BAGUETTE SLICES RUBBED WITH A LITTLE RAW GARLIC
THE RESERVED LOBSTER TAIL MEAT, CHOPPED

- HEAT THE BISQUE IN THE DOUBLE BOILER. FILL WIDE
  SHALLOW WHITE BOWLS WITH THE HOT BISQUE. TOP EACH
  WITH A SLICE OF TOASTED, GARLIC-RUBBED BAGUETTE AND 2
  TABLESPOONS FINELY CHOPPED LOBSTER MEAT FROM THE TAIL.

- IF YOU HAVEN'T DEVOURED THE CLAWS, THIS IS A VERY NICE
  LITTLE EXTRA ON A SMALL SIDE PLATE TO OFFER WITH THE
  BISQUE ALONG WITH A TOOL TO CRACK THE CLAW AND A
  LITTLE SHRIMP FORK.

THE END (BUT SEE NOTES AND SHOPPING LIST).

CHEF NOTES

- WHEN THE BISQUE IS FINISHED, IMMEDIATELY PLACE A
  BUTTERED WAXED PAPER CIRCLE, BUTTER SIDE DOWN, ON
  THE TOP OF THE BISQUE AND COVER IT. THIS WILL KEEP
  A SKIN FROM FORMING.

- A FEMALE LOBSTER DIFFERS FROM A MALE LOBSTER IN THIS
  WAY: LOOK AT THE UNDERBELLY SHELL. YOU WILL SEE A
  V-SHAPED PATTERN OF PETALS DOWN BOTH SIDES, POINTING
  DOWNWARDS. REPEAT: THIS IS THE FEMALE.

- ON THE MALE, THE V-SHAPED PATTERN OF PETALS ARE

continued   Lobster Bisque

THICKER AND HEAVIER, AND POINT UPWARD.

☼ THE FEMALE IS SWEETER AND PROVIDES A RED ROE, WHICH
WE CAN USE TO MAKE A SUBTLE DUSTING POWDER.

INGREDIENT LIST

1 $1/2$ POUNDS LIVE MAINE LOBSTER, PREFERABLY FEMALE,
OR 1 $1/2$ POUNDS LOBSTER TAILS IN SHELLS

1 POUND RAW MEDIUM SHRIMP, IN THEIR SHELLS

SALT

12 WHITE PEPPERCORNS

2+ TABLESPOONS, SWEET BUTTER

1 MEDIUM ONION

1 MEDIUM CARROT

1 STALK CELERY

ZEST OF A LEMON

FRESH THYME SPRIGS

6 TABLESPOONS LONG-GRAIN WHITE RICE

1 CUP DRY WHITE WINE

$1/2$ CUP DRY SHERRY (DO NOT BUY "COOKING WINE," IT IS MISER-
ABLE AND SALTY. USE A GOOD BRAND, ONE YOU WOULD DRINK.)

1 CUP HEAVY CREAM

1 CUP LOW-FAT, LOW SODIUM CHICKEN BROTH

4 TABLESPOONS TOMATO PASTE (FROM A TUBE)

$1/4$ TEASPOON CAYENNE PEPPER

BAGUETTE

PEELED GARLIC CLOVES

"We Ready Are
to Try Our Fortunes"

—Henry IV, Part Two

We worked long and hard building the restaurant, day by day, and then I worked all night at Simon's drive-in. We had no employees—just us. It took almost three months to pull everything together. Finally, it was time to send out the invitations.

They went to all of Harry's friends: the movie stars, the writers, the directors, and the tennis players. It was Harry's list only. Herb, my director friend, was out of town on a shoot. So all the faces were new to me, except those I recognized from their films. *I was so happy to be there, so happy to be involved in this project, especially with a man I adored, but barely knew.*

Everyone was invited to come to my newly rented house on Doheny Drive first for cocktails and hors d'oeuvres. The little money I had saved from selling my modeling agency back in Cleveland allowed me to rent a lovely little furnished house, smartly done in Empire décor.

> Harry Lewis
> and
> Marilyn Conrad
> request the pleasure of your company
> at a Cocktail Party given in honor of
> the opening of
> Hamburger Hamlet
> on Friday, the 27th of October
> from 6 to 9 p.m.
> 714 N. Doheny Drive
> R.S.V.P.   CR 1-5980

There was a charming and perfectly manicured yard, with brick paths and shady trees. The month was October and the nights were balmy. The second part of the evening was a secret.

I took on a lot, as usual. The day of our opening party, I put my hair back into a ponytail, put on my jeans and went joyfully into the kitchen. I was ready to cook! Ready to make hundreds of crêpes to be transformed into miniature cheese blintzes. I would serve them in tiny bites, passed around on a silver tray. I multiplied everything times three and was off and running, making the batter for the crêpes. But something was wrong…the stove would not turn on!

I HAD FORGOTTEN TO PAY THE GAS BILL!

The gas company was not about to turn the gas back on until someone showed up with a check the next morning. I pleaded, I begged. I told the man on the phone that we were opening a little restaurant that very night, and that the opening party was at my house, and that guests would be arriving in a few hours! He said he could do nothing about it *"until morning"*!

"I'll feed you for the rest of your life if you turn it on for me today!" The situation was very tense. *He did turn it on, and we did feed him for the rest of his life. The Gas Man came to every opening. He came when he got married. He came back many times with his wife. He came with his kids. The Gas Man was always there…until we didn't see him anymore.*

The first phase of the party was a great success. I passed around the little blintzes and then little cheeseburgers on the silver tray. Everyone oohed and aahed. These were probably the first mini-cheeseburgers ever seen in the universe. Then it was time for the second part of the evening, the riddle: where to go next. Harry made the announcement: "Now drive to 8929 Sunset Boulevard (which was only half a mile up the road) and you will see a small building on the corner of Hilldale. Find a parking place up on the hill and come in."

They still didn't know what was coming. That was the fun of it.

Do you remember Diana Lynn, star of Miracle of Morgan's Creek? She was in many of the photos in Dominick Dunne's scrapbook memories.

She asked me, "Who's in it?"

"Who's in what? I replied.

"In the play?" she insisted.

"The play?" I asked.

"Yes, the parody…you're doing a parody on Hamlet, aren't you?" She continued, 'Hamburger Hamlet!' It's so cute! What time does it start?"

Utterly confused, I walked away.

They all piled in to this little knotty pine Hamlet with thirty seats and the party continued. I hurried back to the kitchen to mind the stove, or I should say, a two-burner hot plate. Orders started coming in. Cheese blintzes, more cheese blintzes, Cherries Jubilee, and more. Just like Lucille Ball trying to keep up on the chocolate assembly line, stuffing chocolates into her mouth and bra, I couldn't keep up! Juggling those two little electric burners! It was a nightmare. Suddenly the place was packed to the rafters. We had a hit on our hands!

But what about me? Help!

When the lights went on inside this tiny establishment, the traffic on the Sunset Strip backed up, and customers descended en masse. We hadn't figured on this. My mathematics were all off, not to mention the two-burner hot plate, which was excruciatingly slow. How would I ever put out all of these ambitious dishes to a packed house?

And there was Harry, out front in his Dick Carroll tattersall vest, blue blazer, and gray flannels. He was shaking hands, posing for pictures, kissing air, and having a ball. I must admit, for a minute I did resent him. No glamour job, mine.

Quaking with fear, minding the frantic stove, and ready to cry, I was suddenly hit with the biggest young star of the day, Tony Curtis! In my kitchen! He

was carrying a dripping wet, empty ice-packed tray, and shouting "More hamburgers quick! More of those perfect hamburgers!"

"We have more buns at my beck than we have hamburgers to put in them…." Shakespeare was talking to me.

As he handed it to me, the tray doused me and my beautiful (seen by no one) little dress, which shrunk the delicate peau-de-soie skirt up so short that I spent the rest

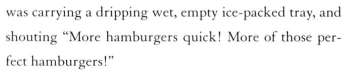

A packed house
at the little
Hamlet.

Photo by Albert Duval.

of the evening wrapped in a butcher's apron, cooking and crying.

When the crowd left, I came out front to the beaming Harry and wailed, "Who, back in Cleveland, will ever believe I was here? All the movie magazines were here and no one thought about me back there covered in *this, this apron!!*"

But the crowd loved it! The warm, homey decor was a social equalizer. No one was better than anyone else. The room had no "good side" and no "bad side." Stars and celebs who were used to the fancy places sat together and mixed with the unemployed actors with great ease. Ava Gardner wrapped in platinum fur would sit up at the little ten-seat counter and nibble on Frank Sinatra's ear. She was a beauty, wearing a pale gray satin pill-box hat with a pearl that dangled down in the center of her high forehead. Sinatra, of course, in a tux.

WHAT A PLACE!

The floors were wood, and on a slant. The whole building slanted. The bathroom consisted of an attached outhouse in the back. Possibly the first unisex facility ever. The entrance was a very narrow pair of screen doors, forcing one to enter sideways and get slapped on the behind by the other door. In the summer months, mushrooms sprouted forcibly between the pine wall boards in the dining room ("Don't eat the mushrooms, please, they are poisonous.") A narrow patio was added, and this brought the European emigrés out. With that came the fans, dancing all over the sidewalks and trying to get the attention of

"MARILYN, ARE YOU SURE YOU CAN COOK?" HE ASKED

"someone" up on the patio. Famous director Michael Curtiz (*Casablanca*) sat with Hollywood columnist Sidney Skolsky, writing *The Eddie Cantor Story* every afternoon. Sometimes, Sidney sat with Greta Garbo, Marlene Dietrich, or Rita Hayworth. Sidney wrote the column "Hollywood Is My Beat," and he was beating the drums for our little place regularly. I thought all the gawking fans were bad for business. To this day we protect the famous, to the best of our ability. *A little comfort and privacy can be a precious thing.* So, with pen in hand and great naivete, I wrote to Sidney Skolsky to ask him to stop writing so much about us. We were getting too popular, I explained to him. He stopped. In the world of public relations, you couldn't buy that kind of publicity. His words were worth a lot. But I was fiercely protective of our little business, and our big customers.

Photo by Albert Duval.   OUR FIRST ANNIVERSARY.

"To Eat or not to Eat:" Hamlet contemplates a cheeseburger.

Polonius to Laertes: "This above all: to Cheese Blintzes be true."

The most engaging and famous people stood in front of our menu board, heads up. In deep concentration, they would choose their hamburger and a side order, aptly named "Eat the Sides, I Pray You." The walls were adorned with little stage sets made of papier-mâché, depicting scenes from *Hamlet*, under glass. The bastardized quotes delighted the thespian crowd. They'd read the menu and the stage quotes aloud for all the crowd to hear.

Because everyone was having so much fun with our take on Shakespeare, I took it a little further. Harry always said, "Don't encourage her!" But I couldn't stop my mind from juxtaposing all the soliloquies and passages I could think of. My mind would ceaselessly talk back in some mixed-up Shakespearean-ese. "Hamlet to the Chef" was most popular—all the great English actors: Robert Newton, Michael Wilding, and Stewart Granger would bellow it out between quaffs and bites…and if they were slightly on the whisky side, it sounded even better! (Margaret Truman carried away many tiny napkins printed with this silly soliloquy.)

Sidney Rushakoff, an artist who traded art for food, painted the wall with me dressed as Ophelia and Harry as Hamlet. The scroll beneath read "Nymphs in thy horizon, may all my hamburgers be remembered."

"As thou art a gourmet, give me the dog. Let go, by heaven, I'll have't."

HAMLET TO THE CHEF

BROIL, the Burger, I pray you, as I pronounced it to you, trippingly on the tongue; but if you burn it, as many broiler men do, I had as lief the physician broil my foods. Nor do not season the morsel too much with thy condiments, thus; but use all gently: for with the hearth's torrid embers, and, as I may say, ingenuity of your profession, you must acquire and beget a temperance and flavor that may give it smoothness.

AYE, there be chefs that I have seen cook, and heard others praise, and that highly, though they be not the gourmet, not to speak it profanely, but the gourmand.

AND it offends me to the soul to see a balloon-pated chef o'ercook a burger to tatters, to very rags, leaving to offend the palate of the epicure, nothing but the charred groundling.

AND if treated with an elfin touch—how capable of succulence!
I would have such a Chef whipped for despoiling the art of the caterer. Pray you, avoid it!

CHEF: I warrant your honor, Prince Hamlet.

BE not too tame neither, but let your own discretion be your tutor; suit the herbs to the spices and the spices to the herbs; with this special observance that you o'erstep not the essence of the flavor; for anything so overdone exposes your oxen-hand!

The purpose both at first and now, was and is, to hold, as t'were, the interest of our gourmet!

Every night stars like Jeff Chandler and Sammy Davis, Jr., decorated the little room. Jeff was unlike a "typical" movie star, in the sense that he wasn't quirky or moody or standoffish. He was friendly, rather quiet, and completely married (unless you believe the recent account written by Esther Williams in her tell-all book). One day I learned a hard lesson. A Hollywood columnist asked me what stars had been in lately. I accidentally mentioned Jeff Chandler being in "and Viveca Lindfors" and it appeared

"ODE TO THE CHEF."

in print, as if they were together. They were not together at all, they were at separate tables, at the same time…. I suffered the slings and arrows of terrible guilt because I told it wrong, I misspoke. Jeff and his wife, Marge, were very forgiving. They understood how such a thing could happen. From then on we taught our management staff (particularly bartenders and hosts) how to "dialogue" properly about celebrities and guests. Perfect example: You never say to a customer, "When you were in yesterday with your wife…." There were new rules to learn. I learned to smile and shut up.

DOROTHY MALONE, ARTHUR KENNEDY,
HARRY (STANDING), ZACHARY SCOTT, AND
RONNIE REAGAN.

RONNIE, HARRY, AND
DOROTHY MALONE.

"LET ME TELL THE WORLD"

—Henry IV, Part One

One night Sarah Churchill came in and refused to give up her glass of beer at the legal witching hour of 2:00 A.M. She called Harry, "You dusty American!" for wanting to take her beer from her. Someone who was there at the time called it into the *International Herald Tribune,* and the next morning we were in every paper in the nation, and in several countries. Suddenly, we were on the map. From that night on, it was S.R.O. every night. No one could stop the flow of publicity.

We were constantly running out of cheese blintzes. "Freeze them." Tenner said, "Thanks a lot, Ruth." More expense...

Business was good. Harry was banking the money and saving it. It wasn't very much—maybe $75 to $100 per day—but Harry was saving it and he wasn't enthusiastic about spending it.

Not only would we have to hire someone to help me make all those blintzes, but now we would have to buy a freezer. Thank God for Sears & Roebuck's lay-away plan.

It was becoming clear that we had to get some help. Harry's mother, Grandma Pauline, helped out by washing the dishes and Harry manned the grill, occasionally relieved by two moonlighting actors.

At two in the morning, the place was filled with young gay men (or gay young men, as we said then) and whenever Dan Dailey came in they would all scream, "Oh Mizzz Dailey," and dance around the room with their hands on their hips, mincing like mad! It was very embarrassing for the poor man, and I didn't understand any of it.

DAN DAILEY

At the time, I was too tired and pregnant to be very thrilled about our new fame. Sudden fame scared me. *Excessive popularity had to be thought through.* We wanted it to last, not to be a flash in the pan.

Great show business talents such as Bobby Short, the Fred Astaire of saloon singers and Cole Porter incarnate, would come to the Hamlet after his show, late at night. Bobby was appearing at the Café Gala on the Sunset Strip (years later, the same site became Wolfgang Puck's first Spago).

Everyone who was anyone, my dear, came to the Gala to hear Bobby. Exiled royalty, movie stars, and studio moguls, including the real Cole Porter. Bobby sang "Just One of Those Things," "My Romance," and "Just a Gigolo." We went as often as we could get away. (He mentions his visits with us in his book *The Saloon Singer.*)

When Bobby sang, you were quiet. You listened. No one commanded that kind of attention except Ella Fitzgerald. No one but no one is like "The Bobby." To hear him perform one of his fanciful double entendres is rich, like:

"And when all your neighbors are upper class, you won't know your Joneses from your Ass-tors." or "When we all have ermine and plastic teeth, how will we determine who's who underneath?"

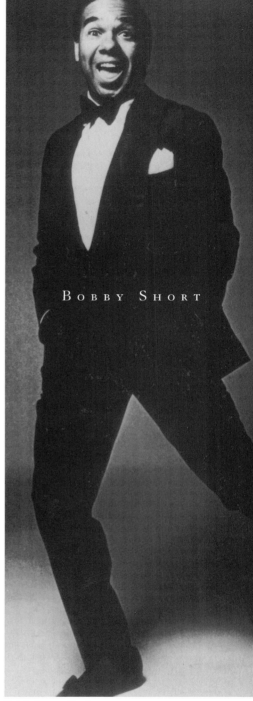

BOBBY SHORT

Photo by Francesco Scavullo.

Thirty-some years later, in 1989, Bobby appeared in a film I produced *Superstar: The Life and Times of Andy Warhol,* because Andy had drawn his feet.

Well, you know Andy. You never knew what Andy was going to draw.

Sammy Davis, Jr. was appearing at Ciro's on the Sunset Strip and the audience was eating him up. His last show ended at 1:00 A.M., which put him and his backstage pals at the Hamlet by about 2:30 A.M. It was quite something to see him pour sugar on a redwood table, jump up there, and do a soft-shoe. The audience in the Hamlet was ecstatic. All that energy! I never saw him tired.

Not like us. We were tired all the time, and yet, somehow we had energy to work, work, work.

SAMMY REMAINED A GREAT FRIEND UNTIL THE END OF HIS LIFE.

When an order for cheese blintzes or Cherries Jubilee came in, I'd have to lift the 5-gallon pot of barbecue sauce off the burner (it took all my might). Then on would go the sauté pan. When that was finished, back would go the big pot of barbecue sauce. This went on every day, day after day. If it wasn't barbecue sauce, it was chili. My arms ached.

A reporter interviewed me about our overnight popularity:

"How did it make you feel when the crowds were overflowing outside of your restaurant and customers had to eat sitting on a stoop?"

"Like it was a bubble that would burst. It scared me."

"What did you do about it?"

"I wrote to Hollywood columnist Sidney Skolsky (first to discover Lana Turner sitting at Schwab's drugstore), and asked him to stop writing about us." *An unheard-of move.*

CHERRIES JUBILEE

SIMPLE. FIRST, BE SURE EVERYONE IS IN THEIR SEATS (IF THE ICE CREAM MELTS FROM THE HEATED CHERRIES, IT'S SOUP). OPEN A CAN OF BING CHERRIES, AND HEAT THEM, JUICE AND ALL, AND ADD A LITTLE BURGUNDY WINE, A TOUCH OF PORT, A SLICE OF LEMON, A DASH OF CINNAMON, AND A DASH OF SUGAR. LADLE SOME OF THE HOT AND BUBBLY MIXTURE OVER AND AROUND TWO SCOOPS OF RICH VANILLA ICE CREAM IN A BEAUTI-FUL HEAVY GLASS DISH. (I USED TO GET THE CUSTOMERS OFF THE PAY PHONE OR OUT OF THE REST ROOM TO GET THEM TO THE TABLE ON TIME BEFORE EVERYTHING MELTED. IT HAD TO BE A LA MINUTE!)

"You did that?" She was amazed. "Do you have a business left???"

"We do now," I answered.

"…And how did you manage that? It doesn't seem like a restaurant that enjoys a late-night reputation could pull that one off, especially on the Sunset Strip!"

"By closing earlier. By changing the 3 A.M. closing time to 2 A.M. There were too many crazies at that hour… then we added a baked potato."

"…Added a baked potato? What did that do?" the reporter asked.

"Well, my thought was that if our Beverly Hills clientele saw the late-late crowd, who were crazy-crazy, they wouldn't think of The Hamlet as a place for dinner. A place where they could have a baked potato at dinnertime—you do understand I'm using the baked potato as a metaphor, don't you?"

"Hmmm. Yes, go on…" she said.

"The crowd was very bohemian and theatrical. It was much looser late at night. I wanted it to settle down a bit. Make it more substantial, like a baked potato at dinnertime feels. You know how that feels… soothing." I told her.

"Well, I guess it is… I never thought of it that way…."

"The problem with putting a baked potato in for dinner," I told her, "was that we didn't have an oven. So I called Tenner."

"Who is Tenner?"

"My best friend," I answered.

"What did she say?"

She said, "Buy an oven." *So once again we were faced with a capital expenditure.* "Harry was not for the added expense, but when I polled our guests they all signed up for a baked potato. By popular demand, we won."

So off to Sears we went, to find a new stove. A four-burner gas one with a little oven. It fit the space and was perfect! And the dinner business with the baked potato started to increase.

"Wow, what a crash course in marketing I've just had!" The reporter said.

"Thou Art an Elm, My Husband; I, a Vine"

—The Taming of the Shrew

Our life was all work. Until one night Jeff Chandler, Sammy Davis, Jr., and Tony Curtis sat us down with a plan. A plan for us to get married.

The idea of getting married was just something else we had no time to think about. Jeff was married, Tony was about to marry Janet Leigh, and Sammy was going with Mai Britt. Seeing the two of us joined at the hip, as we were, it was assumed we were married (and if we weren't, we *should* be). Living together was never discussed out loud, yet, by that time we *were* living together. We were partners in every sense of the word. Just partners without papers. It was not an issue (rather strange in the '50s). Going home together and going to work together was just what we did.

We were touched by their offer, to put it mildly. Imagine three major talents offering to hang out and cook for the customers for a night or two, just so we could go to Las Vegas and tie the knot. It was like a sit-com. How could we refuse?

JEFF CHANDLER AND BYRON KANE
(A WELL-KNOWN VOICE ON THE RADIO) WORK
THE COUNTER WHILE WE GOT MARRIED.

Those three guys not only pushed us out to get married, but actually broiled the hamburgers, took the orders, and rang up the money—and gave no autographs for two days while we were in Las Vegas.

Las Vegas was a long drive. I drove while Harry slept. He was tired from working so many hours. It was very late when we arrived. Driving down the Strip we saw many wedding chapels. "Maybe tomorrow," we thought. But then we decided to wake up the little man who played minister.

We got married.

Our friend
David Wolper.

Later, I would joke, "We had to get married—where else was Harry going to find a partner like me?"

Everyone had to come into the tiny little kitchen and see my new stove. Shelley Winters, Tony Curtis, Rock Hudson, and the young David Wolper. They all stared at it and didn't know quite what to say....

Shelley Winters was a really big star when we were slaving away at our first little restaurant. She apparently had just had her teeth capped and felt she had to show them to everyone. "Look! Look!" she'd say, as she'd pull the corners of her mouth open. "Aren't they wonderful!" Then she stuck her finger into my mouth, running it across my molars, asking loudly, "Do you have all your

own teeth?" Nothing embarrassed Shelley... she was always right up front. I showed her my new stove, she showed me her new teeth.

At closing time, Zachary Scott, the quirky, handsome 1950s Warner Brothers star often appeared. He starred in *Mildred Pierce* with Joan Crawford, and Harry had worked with him in *Her Kind of Man,* with Dane Clark and Janis Paige.

"Is it too late to order?" he'd ask, coming through half of the swinging door, while the other one hit him in the backside. "Not for you. A number 7 meejum rare, and a glass of milk?" We would ask.

"Thanks, where's the broom?"

While we broiled, he'd sweep. What a sweet man this was. Actually, I found most of the stars of that period to be like this. Helpful, gentle, and very approachable. Tony Curtis, Rock Hudson, Debbie Reynolds, Cesar Romero, Edward G. Robinson. There were only a few who were standoffish.

One night Zachary arrived with Joan Crawford on his arm. They were working together shooting *Sudden Fear* (1952), which earned an Oscar nomination for her. "Joan did her best climbing-up-the-wall scene today," he said, "so they let her out to have a hamburger with me." He had a very acerbic sense of humor. He also wore an earring.

Now when I watch her films, I see what he meant. She positions herself against the wall, spreads her arms and chews up the scenery. She won an Academy Award for that wall-climbing routine in her role as *Mildred Pierce* (also with Zachary Scott) and a first Oscar nomination for *Possessed* in 1947.

She told us, while Zachary swept, that the story of *Mildred Pierce* was almost the same as ours, except for the murder, of course. I said, "I hope your conclusion is accurate, Miss Crawford." Still watching Zachary sweep, she asked, "Does he do this often?"

One day Zachary asked if I would cater a party at his apartment, for his new film *The Secret of Convict Lake.* I was very excited about doing it, and do it I did, all alone.

I shopped all morning at Hazen's and paid almost $200 for groceries. It was my first catering job. When the guests arrived, I remember sitting in the corner of the dining room, and watching the food on the table disappear within 15 minutes. I was so tired I couldn't move. We were totally wiped out in 15 minutes! That was the end of catering for me. And to make matters worse, he never asked me for the bill. So there wasn't one.

Not too profitable. Working actors never seem to pay for a thing. They have business managers to do that, only I didn't know who he was....

ZACHARY SCOTT AND JOAN CRAWFORD IN *Mildred Pierce.*

Photo from *Mildred Pierce* © 1945 Turner Entertainment Co. A Time Warner Co. All Rights Reserved.

DRESSER DAHLSTAT OF ABC CALLING...

Since we had no help at the Hamlet, we thought it expedient to put in a microphone. I could use my special "Lauren Bacall" voice to call out the orders as they came up. Everyone was intrigued to see who arrived to pick up the order, especially when the name was "Smith." Most celebrities left the name "Smith" or "Johnson," with a little wink of the eye. We'd say, "Thank you, Mr. Smith," to Jack Benny, Ray Milland, Paul Douglas, Tab Hunter, Tony Curtis, or Rock Hudson. "Thank you, Miss Smith" to Debbie Reynolds, Marlene Dietrich, Doris Day, Janet Leigh, Rita Hayworth, or Greta Garbo. Marilyn Monroe always left her own name and wiggled away with her tray. Some came just to hear my sultry voice, or so they said. Well, come they did, and one day my sultry voice paid off.

I received a call from a Mr. Dresser Dahlstat of ABC Broadcasting. *You couldn't make up a name like that.* He asked who the voice was on the microphone at the Sunset Hamlet. I told him it was me. He asked if I would be interested in auditioning for a radio show called "The Farmer's Daughter," as a disc jockey. I thought this voice was fooling me. Finally, I came to and listened.

The hours on air would be long: midnight to 5:30 in the morning, five nights a week. *It was not as if I had nothing else to do, but the money would be welcome....* I told him I'd never done anything like this in my life, but he encouraged me. He said that if I could sound so sexy announcing that an order was ready, I would certainly pass the test. I was scared, but beginning to learn that determination pays off.

I listened to the radio to see how the other announcers sounded. Learned the cadence and the feeling of a smooth segue. And got the job! What a break that was for us. We were so fiscally deprived that we had a fifteen dollar lamp on hold at the May Company.

Now money was coming in every week. For us, it was Big Money. Harry kept a little radio on our ten-seat counter; while he broiled the late nights away, he made everyone listen to his wife and her low, dulcet tones. The funniest part of the whole adventure was that I wore a mask. On the radio! My identity was to be hidden until they were ready to unmask me. The publicity was great for the show.

It was Jay Livingston, the great songwriter, who said I had a great face for radio.

I think it was Army Archerd of *Variety* who first let the face out of the mask. A publicity stunt.

While I gave birth to our first son, David, Tony Curtis, Jeff Chandler, and Sammy Davis, Jr., took over the Sunset Hamlet again, broiling those burgers, taking cash, and taking orders, so that Harry could be with me.

These three famous guys did this for us when we got married and here they were again when we were having our first child. Harry was late arriving but ecstatic that he had a son. *Things were so different then. There were no birthing classes, and no amniocentesis procedure. Everything was a surprise.*

Harry used to close the Hamlet at 3:00 A.M., and after he swept up and counted the money, he would drive down to Studio A at Hollywood and Vine and fall asleep on the piano bench, waiting for the end of my broadcast.

I truly loved being on the air, but having to cook every day at our restaurant didn't make for an easy life.

Once my (two) thirteen-week contract periods were over, I returned to work at the little Hamlet full-time along with taking care of our little boy, David. But something new had happened on the boulevard. A former disk jockey had opened a spot called My Own Place, and he was stealing our thunder! He had a radio wire inside his restaurant.

"Why can't we have a radio wire too?" I asked Harry (never one to sit around on my sesame seed buns). I had already done twenty-six weeks on the air as "The Farmer's Daughter," so I knew how. Immediately he blocked me with the expense.

"Let's just find out how much a wire costs." He argued.

"We could get it sponsored, couldn't we?" I pleaded.

We talked to KGIL. Armed with the facts, Harry went out and got the sponsors. They were Mad Man Muntz TV, Singer Triumph Sports Cars, and Seaboard Finance Co.

The sponsors' money met the expense of the wire and the engineer we needed, so it was a wash. The show was called *Hollywood at The Hamlet.* It brought all our late customers back. For short, everyone called the show "Hare and Mare on the Air." We said stupid funny things to each other… arcane things like, "You go broil and I'll save France." *Now what the hell does that mean?* Unless you're from the '50s and you've heard Mel Brooks and Carl Reiner's uproarious LP "The 2000-Year Old Man," you wouldn't have a clue. When the restaurant got "wrapped" (meaning overly busy), Harry would step down from the mike and go to the broiler to get those hamburgers out, while I was left on the mike alone.

One night a man called in to say, "When I listen to you two, it sounds like I'm eavesdropping on a married couple and I shouldn't be." *I still don't know if that was good or bad.* At that time the famous "couple" on the air were "Tex and Jinx" out of New York. If we sounded like them, fine. They certainly did everything to make you feel you were eavesdropping on their lives. Our show was on from midnight till 2:00 in the morning, so we had a lot of time to fill. We never knew who would be around, so there had to be a lot of husband-and-wife talk between us. We sat up high at a corner table and whenever we spotted someone of note we would ask them to come up. They'd act like they weren't interested, but oh yes, they were! Peggy Lee, Joan Crawford, Lana Turner, Gig Young, Olivia de Havilland, Rock Hudson, Doris Day, among others. Everyone enjoyed being on. When we were so tired we couldn't speak, we'd ask Sammy Davis, Jr. or any big celebrity in the room to take over the show for us and he would. No one refused.

Occasionally, when we were really busy cooking, we would have to play a record or two in between, which brought out the "record pluggers." It was all slightly crazy, but wonderful fun.

Jay Livingston (famous writer of "Buttons and Bows," "Mona Lisa," "Mr. Ed") reminisced recently about how sorry he felt for us then, working so hard broadcasting and cooking at the same time. He told us he sat at work on the Paramount lot worrying about bringing in enough people that night to provide an audience for the show. "You had me worried." He said. "I thought I had to fill the room for you." At the time, Jay was writing all the music for the Bing Crosby and Bob Hope movies and was worrying about us. It was a love affair.

But the time came when I knew I would have to stay at home much more, to care for our baby.

ON THE AIR

SAMMY DAVIS, JR. ON THE AIR, WITH HUGH O'BRIAN, MARILYN, AND HARRY.

CESAR ROMERO, MARILYN, AND HARRY.

JOSEPH KAUFMAN (PRODUCER OF *Sudden Fear)*, HIS WIFE DORIS DANIELS, AND NANCY KELLY, STAR OF STAGE AND SCREEN.

"Go to the Wonderful Pullman Waiters and Ask Them Where the Women Are"

We simply had to hire some people to help us. Something told me, "Go to the men who used to work on the Santa Fe SuperChief." I knew about some of the retired ones who worked at a high-priced chop house on La Cienega, called the Tail of the Cock. *My destiny was coming to pass — my angel was guiding me.* I thought perhaps we could hire their daughters, their cousins, their wives…good, honest people with a strong work ethic.

I went to see these men. I began: "Our menu can't offer the tips you make here, but if we could meet your daughters, your wives, maybe your sisters…." *Hattie was very near to me now.* The men chuckled among themselves and shook their heads. One of them said, "These girls don't have much education, and some of them can't do the arithmetic."

"Send them to me, please. As long as they can speak English and read I will teach them," I urged.

"They can't add up a check." More chuckling and head-shaking.

"There are adding machines that can do that job," I said. "Please," I begged. "Where are they working now?"

They were day-workers, some doing laundry, housekeepers, maids.

"Send them to me, please."

My motivation had nothing to do with the color of a person's skin—I wanted to bring people into my dream. People I felt were missing from the American Dream.

The waiters sent their women en masse and the new waitress school began. First, we had to select a role model. It was so strange—they didn't have one. Someone suggested Grace Kelly because she was so elegant. They liked her because she walked tall and her hair was done up so neatly. So we plucked and arched eyebrows, we used depilatories for unneeded hair, softened makeup, and the girls did walk proudly. They were hungry for this kind of attention and loved learning. Almost as much as I loved teaching them.

PLUCKING EYEBROWS.

"ANGRY" EYEBROWS.

"SURPRISED" EYEBROWS.

It took me back to teaching at my modeling school in Cleveland. It was an epiphany for me to realize that I had never seen a black model, or interviewed a black woman for starting such a career. There was this whole segment of women missing from the workplace. Divine intervention was at work here, and it all came from Hattie. Being with these girls reminded me so strongly of her.

My grandmother and I had positively identified Hattie's body at the County Morgue. Because she was drunk, and happened to be deaf, she didn't hear the horn of a taxi that came barreling down the street. The driver ran her over and dragged her twenty-five feet. She was wearing my grandmother's fur, in which we buried her at a proper service in Potter's Field. I was only ten, and shattered. But Hattie's spirit was always with me, from then on.

Esther Crayton was one of these fine young women, and she expressed herself to us in a letter years later. She told how the girls had never felt comfortable crossing the racial barrier to work west of Western Avenue. That we had opened avenues for them to travel on more than just the streets. *Thirteen years later the Civil Rights Act was passed into law. The law told the people that equal is equal, underscoring that racial boundaries were now gone forever.* I wish that were true.

The word was out that the Hamlet was a great place to work.

Our new waitress school was like a finishing school: Diction and elocution, poise, suggestive selling, makeup, grooming, and voice modulation. *Subjects I had to learn in order to be a Junior Miss model.*

We taught the staff how to finesse our upscale clientele while serving the lowly but delicious Hamburger. *"No one was to feel any angst or stress when they came through our doors. Not the customers. Not the waitresses."*

I told them: "If someone doesn't leave a tip, you must consider that they may have just been fired from their job. They may have had a fight with their loved one. They may be in the throes of a divorce. Any number of things could have happened. It is our job to ease their pain. Make everything smooth for them. If you have to cry, go to the rest room, but show the customer a happy smile."

The original course lasted six weeks, much longer than it needed to be, but I was enjoying it so much and the girls never wanted it to end. It attracted the press in very positive ways. Long before McDonald's Hamburger U., more like a fine finishing school for girls. We held some of the classes in the dining room of our home.

Before there was the passing of a Civil Rights Bill, before there was Martin Luther King, Jr., there was Marilyn Lewis, Harry Lewis, and Hamburger Hamlet. Mr. and Mrs. Lewis, you were practicing civil rights, enhancing and enriching the lives of so many, including myself.

You didn't talk about it, you didn't broadcast it, you didn't televise it, you just did it. There you were, opening doors to us who could go no other place and be employed as a waitress because of the color of our skin. When I came to you, Western Avenue was as far west as we could go and Washington Boulevard was as far north as we could go. Yes, there were men who were waiters in the dinner houses but women of color had no place to go. What a tremendous blessing you all have been by touching so many lives in a positive and productive manner.

Esther Crayton

ESTHER CRAYTON

Art Seidenbaum of the *Los Angeles Times* was riveted by the classes. Later, he wrote a wonderful essay, which we had printed on white napkins and used as a liner under our fried chicken in a basket. I'm sure he was pleased.

'Do we ever use the word "fried"?' said owner-trainer Marilyn Lewis to nearly thirty new aspiring Hamlet ladies.

'No', chorused the would-be waitresses, 'we say "sautéed."'

"For these eager students, it was the third intensive day of a seven-day training class administered to each of 350 people who man and woman the most exalted hamburger stands in the Western world....

"The beginnings were Bohemian (sic) actor Harry Lewis (regarded as a great baby-faced killer at a time when there was no market for baby-faced killers), was looking for a quiet place where other actors and writers might chew on their frustrations.

"He had his irreverent, alliterative name, which combined the great tragedy of the English language with the ruling passion of the American stomach. He also had an ambitious girlfriend named Marilyn, who would even cook publicly if he would marry her. In 1950, the wedding of all elements.

"The girls are drilled: Each, in turn, practiced the haunting line: "While you're waiting would you like some of our delicious lobster bisque or some French onion soup fondue?" And as they rehearsed for the Brentwood opening Mrs. Lewis offered cues: "Sing it a little bit," and "Can you say 'fondue' without blinking both eyes?" and "If you don't smile when you say that, Tina, your magic will be lost."

"The Hamlet method is that graciousness, more than speed, matters. Each waitress in indoctrinated with the notion that she is in business for herself even as she serves the meat-and-potato purposes of the management. It appears to work. Hamlet grads earn between $100 and $150 a week and almost never quit.

"Bohemia died of success. Hamlets moved uptown into Westwood, Beverly Hills, downtown into the financial district, then into the family way of the San Fernando Valley...."

—**Art Seidenbaum**, *Los Angeles Times*, **December 10, 1963**

"A Kickass Tale"

Esther reminded me of the time two of the girls got into it, and called each other black bitches and said they were going to kick ass. I didn't encourage that street talk, and we seldom heard it. "You called a meeting," Esther said, "that very night and opened with 'Listen up everyone! I'm the black bitch here and no one can kick ass like I can, because this is my business, not yours, and until it is your business, you're going to have to talk things out in a calm manner. We're all ready to listen to everyone here. So if anyone is kicking ass, let's start talking about it right here, *now!*"

"Then we all hugged and went home." She concluded.

The truth is that I didn't speak that way or think that way, but at the time it seemed that, if I could pick up on their lingo to stop this sniveling rivalry, and become one with them, it might get my point across. It certainly did. It was transactional. And it was good.

"Everyone knew you had a capacity for forgiveness but they knew not to cross the line," Esther said. "Nothing infuriated you more than when we didn't get along with each other. You cut out a lot of petty quarreling. Coexisting with co-workers was paramount to you," said Esther.

No one ever needed to be fired. They just had to hear the word and know where the management stood. We even discussed Governor Wallace of Alabama, a racist segregationist. Why him? Many of the girls expressed how they respected his views because he was, at least, honest. I learned so much from them. Behavioral science was a big subject with us. The year? 1955.

Unfortunately, ten years later Watts would erupt in flames.

SEND YOUR CHILDREN TO COLLEGE

As soon as we could afford it, Harry took me to New York.

It was 1955. We had heard about the hiring practices of Chock Full of Nuts (they hired only colored* girls to work at the counter). There were signs: "No Tipping Please."

I couldn't figure this out. You never saw a sign like that where men worked as waiters. This was especially puzzling since Brooklyn Dodger Jackie Robinson was a director on their board. He had broken the color barrier in major league baseball in 1947.

*the language of the day

When I came home, I told the girls about this no tipping policy, which I certainly did not agree with. I encouraged them to be as professional as they could be. "Take your tips home," I told them, "and save them to buy a house and send your children to college." This is exactly what they did.

"You can be anything you want to be, you just have to want to do it, and study hard for it." I told them because I believed it. After all, it was working for me.

It was such a pleasure to work with these women. We investigated the origins of the foods we would serve and come to realize that food did indeed bring all people together, as does music. "Crêpes" in France were "blintzes" in Russia. "Stuffed cabbage" in Poland was "choux farci" in France. American hamburgers were really born in Hamburg, Germany (described vividly as "a piece of meat between two slices of cake"). We all loved these classes. *The girls were terrific, and wore their waitress caps like crowns. Hattie was shining down on us every step of the way.*

LEARNING MENU COMPREHENSION.

Marketing:
The $6,000
Baked Apple

On our second trip to New York in 1957, we stayed at the St. Regis. My friend Doris Daniels introduced us to the baked apple at Longchamps. It was served on a beautiful large green magnolia leaf, and baked to perfection. This was years before we began to see such artistry on the plate. We didn't have much money then and the trip was very expensive for us. I asked Harry if we could stay over one more day to try to get the recipe. One more day turned into one more day and one more day—but I did manage to persuade the chef to share the baked apple recipe with me.

When we got back, I practiced and practiced making this apple until I achieved the same perfection. It went on the menu and the guests adored it. The trip had eventually cost $6,000 and naming the apple only added to its popularity. I was learning how to communicate with our customers. They loved knowing the story of the $6,000 baked apple and sharing it with their friends.

Our Buffalo Soldier

William McClendon was a black man who wandered into our lives and took on a very important and trustworthy position. We shared and trusted him with all our secret recipes. He worked for the Hamlets for thirty years and only much later did we learn of the desperate risk he ran to be free. This is his own story of Biloxi, Mississippi, in the '50s.

"I was workin' out at the base, Keester Field, in Biloxi. Workin' as a cook in the mess hall, that fed the medics and the sick people. The year was 1957. We would make the food and one time one of the people in charge, a colonel, a lady, was watchin' me. She asked me if I wanted to cook special food for the white people. One of the sergeants that lived up in Mississippi, well, he had a problem with this colonel lady talkin' to me first. He wanted her to talk to him first. She was very much above him in rank, but he thought because of my color and because he was in charge of the mess hall, she should talk to him first. The sergeant didn't want me to follow any of the colonel's orders. He tried to get me fired. The colonel lady transferred the sergeant instead.

Our Buffalo Soldier.

"When I was gettin' ready to go home, the sergeant and some of his friends were out there waitin' for me. They jumped me and I got hurt some and I ran. The MPs were patrolling the base and picked me up and took me home. I had been cookin' on that base for seven to eight years, all the time since the war. This sergeant started the story that 'something' was goin' on with this colonel lady. I left Biloxi in fear of my life and went to Gulfport, Mississippi. I stayed with my brother, and wondered what to do about my job. I tried to go back and didn't even make it there. As I came through the door at the base, I got jumped by four guys, and that made my mind up. I knew it wouldn't work for me to get killed, so I resigned. I took the bus to my brother's home twelve miles away and I didn't go home anymore. I went to L.A. where I met the Lewises."

William's brother in Biloxi knew the Hamburger Hamlets in L.A. had a good hiring practice and confirmed there were a lot of black people working for them. So William met Harry, *and he was all set up in a new job, as it turned out, for the rest of his life.*

William had a wife, Oleta, and four children still back in Biloxi. He was scared for them because some of those white guys at the base began to terrorize his family. He got his family out in 1960, two years after he started working for us.

In fact, Biloxi was a special case because it was a part of the Keester base, and many businesses were dependent on the airmen. William called them "airma." When the men of color (who had fought for their country in World War II) were denied service at the front window of a business, they decided to eat at the base rather than be subjected to that kind of persecution. Businesses suffered all around the base. The "airma" were not going to go around to the colored window in the back to place their order for something to eat. So business in Biloxi let up and relaxed the rules, in the name of commerce. It got a little better, but only near the base. The rest of Mississippi was a lot worse, for a long time. "A lot of white 'airmas' stood up for the black 'airmas,'" he said, "but a lot of them didn't."

William had been drafted into the army in 1942 and started base training at Camp Stewart, Georgia, in an all-black unit called the Buffalo Division, 92nd Infantry, 1st Army. He was shipped overseas to Glasgow, Scotland; from there, down through England and on to France, where the division blended with white soldiers. He remembers having a white buddy from the South:

"We talked about how we was there to protect one another and we got to talkin' more. He admitted he had hatred in his heart for the Negroes because his parents taught him to. But now, he feels like we was brothers. He could hear his momma, on the farm where he came from, tellin' him that Negro people should be treated like dogs and fed from the back door."

He never went to visit his buddy after the war. He had seen enough of that prejudice and didn't want any more of it. William was given a medal for bravery because he went in while the enemies were flying overhead, and pulled out the guys in trouble. He was honorably discharged in Fort Dix, New Jersey, in 1948. He had served his country well. But when William got home, he couldn't visit his buddy or buy a hamburger at the front window. History does set the table for what you do in life. He made his home at Hamburger Hamlet.

William made just about every one of those $6,000 baked apples. In the early days, he made our home all sweet and sugary-smelling with those apples—our boys still remember that aroma from when they came home from school. I wanted to tell William's story here to shine a deserved light of importance and significance on his life.

- ❦ Core six Roman Beauty or other green apples, then pare them halfway down from the top.

- ❦ Sprinkle 2 tablespoons of sugar on the tops of the peeled apples (1 teaspoon for each one).

- ❦ Place in a pan that holds them snugly. Pour $^1/_4$ cup water per apple into the bottom of pan. Broil under flame of your broiler for 5 minutes only. Do not walk away. The sugar will begin to caramelize and bubble, but do not allow it to burn.

- ❦ Transfer to a 325° oven and bake for 1 hour. Basting twice, like every 20 minutes. If the water evaporates during baking, add more, a few tablespoons at a time.

- ❦ Turn the oven down to 300° for the second hour. Turn baking dish occasionally.

- ❦ Bake for one additional hour at 300°. That's three hours.

- ❦ In the meantime, melt 1 tablespoon apple jelly per apple for the final topping.

- ❦ And in a small saucepan, combine $^1/_2$ cup water and $^1/_2$ cup sugar. Place over low heat and stir until the sugar is dissolved. Keep warm.

- ❦ Place apples on little plates and spoon apple jelly in the center. Spoon a little sugar syrup around the base.

"Marilyn, are you sure you can cook?" he asked

Charlie Feldman
Was No Dummy

It was 1952, only two years after we opened, when we had our first suitor. Mr. Charles Feldman. Big, big Manager, Agent, Producer. The Academy Award-winning film *On The Waterfront* was his. He called to congratulate us on our success and said he'd like to meet with us to make his bid to buy us out. We were in shock. *It never occurred to us that anyone would have such an intention.* We told him we worked all day and into the night, so out of deference to us he actually called the meeting for 3:00 in the morning. We couldn't believe it. He was serious all right. We swept up, counted the money, and went to his office on Wilshire Boulevard in Beverly Hills.

This man was handsome. There he sat in his wood-paneled office behind a large desk, telling us how he admired what we were doing. He offered us $250,000. *More money than we could even fathom.* We just sat there like two lumps.

Then he shocked us by saying, "Isn't that right, Harry?"

And another man named Harry stepped out of the wall! It was his lawyer, Harry Sokoloff, never far from his side. It was 4:00 in the morning and a man steps out of the wall!

We said our first "No. But thank you."

I had never seen anything like this in my life.

From then on we just grew. There were no roadmaps to show the way, but we knew we had something good. *Very good.* Westwood seemed like the right place for us. It was a college town. UCLA, with 15,000 students, and thousands of well-to-do residents. The town was like a quaint village. Someone showed us a worn-out little coffeeshop called Brits, which had outlived its shelf life and closed down. But the lease was still active and very doable for us. The owner wanted "key money." I think we paid him $1,500 hard-earned dollars for the pleasure of this piece of paper. The next problem came when we needed some cash to revamp the place, our way. We simply didn't have it, nor did we have any collateral. Where in the world were we going to get it, when Jack Warner of Warners had turned us down, as well as Gig Young, Cesar Romero, and many other successful actors?

ALL WE NEEDED WAS $5,000

One of our customers was a man named Lou Siegal. He was a banker at the Union Bank, which had the reputation for keeping the "rag" business afloat. We asked if he'd see us concerning a little expansion we wanted to do. He said to come see him and we'd talk about it. *The first loan for our second shop. It was scary.*

"I've watched you. Because you both work so hard, I'm going to recommend to the bank that they give you this loan." It was right out of the film *The Best Years of Our Lives.* Fredric March played a banker who gave small loans without collateral.

Because of this wonderful man, who watched us work and loved our hamburgers, we were able to grow.

Two places made everything seem monumental! I felt dazed and thrilled at the same time. The next problem was who would care for our baby son, David. Since I was expecting our second child, I had to wonder who was going to watch over everything.

LOU SIEGAL: "WHEN MY COLLEAGUES FROWNED ON THE DEAL, I TOLD THEM, 'WHAT THE HELL, IF THEY DON'T PAY US BACK THE $5,000. WHAT'S IT GOING TO DO, BREAK THE BANK?!'"

Westwood Village was like *Mr. Roger's Neighborhood,* but with a white supremacy attitude. *A little-known fact.* The day we opened with a full cast of black waitresses and cooks, tomatoes were hurled at the front windows. *Something I never expected.* I remember the girls all seated at the counter, wearing their starched white blouses, white shoes, and little white crowns on their heads. They were so eager to get started, and then this had to happen. I stood in front of them ready to pop, I was so pregnant, and told them to look at me, not to look at the windows behind me. I told them that when we opened we would change this biased attitude forever. They trusted me, and they did it. Westwood Village was theirs! The people came and they were generous and loving.

Adam was born a few days after we opened and, like a peasant in the field, I went back to work to watch over everything, while Harry worked between the two shops. It was beginning to be hard.

I knew I had to make a call to my mother back in Cleveland. That was clear. Having her here would mean that he *would have to come too. JJ. Hmmm… that was something to consider. But if I thought too much about how he treated me growing up, or how the whole thing would play out, it would have stopped me. Knowing my mother loved him and sensing how much I needed to feel a family around me, I made the call.*

JJ looked like Adolphe Menjou. A very dapper movie star of the '30s and '40s. A man with a superb taste for the moustache and the bow tie. He became the finest front-door person a business could have. The customers loved him and he loved the attention. The movie stars hugged him and brought presents for him on his birthday. He had an innate sense of old Hollywood and to find this at a place called Hamburger Hamlet was unique, to say the least. It got easier for me to call him "Daddy" and Harry called him "JJ." And we all began calling Harry "HL."

We were no longer serving in baskets and paper; we were now a full-blown restaurant but just different enough to be noticed. We were meticulous about everything we did. The food, the cleanliness, the grooming, the attitude, yet above all we were warm and generous. We treated this place as if it were a

MY OFFICE WAS OUTSIDE ON THE SIDEWALK DURING CONSTRUCTION.

OUT WITH THE OLD. IN WITH THE NEW.

private country club dining room and *everyone belonged.*

This was new to everyone. We couldn't be called a coffeeshop. It was simply known as the "Hamlet in Westwood." The most affluent and intellectual people were at home here.

Next Stop:
Bedford Drive, Beverly Hills

We grew like "Topsy," I always say, because we had no plan. If we saw an empty store, we investigated it. Without money, that's about all you can do, unless you take on partners, which we were loath to do. Or unless a landlord decides to build for you, and that's what happened next. It was 1956 and Beverly Hills was an incorporated city with its own fire department, mayor, police force, and tax base. A very wealthy area of about 35,000 people. The general political attitude was liberal and very giving (except for the curfews and the questioning that the police put strangers through if they were driving or walking through the streets at night).

> "What raised the Hamlets out of burger class was cleanliness down to the micro-mote (sic) and the sort of service you used to get in the best hotels.... 'It is show-business, you know,' admitted the proprietress while her students were busy trying to write down all the menu's meatless items from memory, 'and this is no off-Broadway operation.'"
> —Art Seidenbaum, *Los Angeles Times*, December 10, 1963

It was what you would call a "safe neighborhood."

Bedford Drive was a very important street, part residential and part commercial. Saks Fifth Avenue and I. Magnin were just half a block away, up the prestigious Wilshire Boulevard. There were shoppers, residents, and salespeople, all nearby. (This was the extent of our marketing study—it just felt good.) We met Mr. Lerner of Lerner Dress Shops, who reminded me of Sidney Greenstreet (the big man in the big white suit in *The Maltese Falcon*). He owned all the Lerner Dress Shops across the country and many buildings on Bedford Drive. We got lucky, because he was very kind to us. He loved what we had done in

Westwood and decided to "build to suit." This meant that he would put up a certain amount of money for us to build something wonderful. The rent he imposed and a share of profits would pay him back. *Royally.*

This was our first big business bullet and we bit it. But we knew his investment wouldn't cover all the expenses, so we had to put up our recently acquired little home as collateral. We were expanding again, and it was getting scarier and scarier. *Unless you have done this, there's no way to imagine how frightening it is.* Building Westwood a year and half before had been small potatoes compared to Bedford Drive. Our overall bill at Bedford Drive was more than $200,000. My optimism, based on raw courage and a willingness to do whatever it took, was fierce. *We were not going to lose our home!*

One of the largest expenses for a new restaurant, aside from the tabletop and opening-day inventory, is the electrical and plumbing. In Westwood we had inherited the old wiring and pipes. Here at Bedford Drive there was nothing. We had to start from scratch. Also, this time I wanted to build Mr. Mitty's dream house. After all, it was Beverly Hills. Nothing could be too good for these fine people, I felt, even if we couldn't afford it.

We were putting on a show and it was going to be a good one.

Bedford Drive was perfect in every detail. The lines were uniform, symmetrical. The décor: simple, like a fine library. We used book-matched walnut paneling above the red tufted, leather booths. White silk walls atop walnut wainscoting led into the linear space. It felt like a starched white shirt under a fine pinstripe suit. The chandeliers were custom-made black iron with gleaming crystal shades and a little brass trim. The carpet was a happy sunflower design, loomed in various shades of red with purple. George Cameron, a well-known Texas oil man, once said to us, "You keep these places like a gentleman's handkerchief drawer."

The celebrities continued to come. On some days, it seemed everyone you could name was at this Hamlet, reading the paper or a magazine and leisurely enjoying their late lunch.

Bedford Drive was Psychiatrist Row, which certainly played a part in our afternoon popularity. Bedford Drive: the street of the famous Daniel Ellsworth break-in during Watergate *(The Pentagon Papers)*. The street where the Menendez brothers unexpectedly confessed to their psychiatrist.

My artistic bent started with plate presentations. We had added an oak-planked hamburger steak to the menu, and I thought it should be served on an oak plank. Not the usual ones that one could buy from the restaurant supply houses, but a triangular board made of oak and divided for the hamburger steak with onions, the baked potato, and the salad. It was a stunner, and looked twice the price.

However, from a restaurateur's point of view the cost of these planks was even more stunning. They were honed by special machinery. They would split after going through the dishwasher. They would split if they were soaked too long in water. They would split if they were handwashed. But I wouldn't give up on them. Not even for profits. Profits could have been greater, but I wanted the aesthetic to prevail.

For the French onion soup topping, we had a little oven created with a very expensive warming bulb. It melted and bubbled the cheese so beautifully that soon we had to have four more made to keep up with the demand.

For our male guests, we put in a Papa-sized cup and a Mama-sized cup for the gals. Corny as it may seem, it was a conversation piece and we had everyone talking. Hot chocolate mugs were inscribed with the words "The Bedford Hamlet" in gold Spencerian script. Beer mugs were frosted. It was visually stimulating.

DOTTY SPEARS

A much richer version of the one Ann-ma made so simply with just a bone.

1/2 cup sweet butter

4 large onions, sliced very thin

1 teaspoon Dijon mustard

Black pepper

3 quarts (12 cups) defatted brisket broth, or 6 cups
      canned beef broth mixed with 6 cups water

4 beef bouillon cubes dissolved in 1 cup water (do not use
      bouillon cubes if using canned beef broth)

1 1/4 cups Chablis or other dry white wine

12 slices (1/4-inch thick) French bread

1/4 cup applejack brandy

1 1/2 cups freshly grated Parmesan cheese

6 ounces Muenster cheese, cut into 12 thin slices

6 ounces Gruyere cheese, cut into 12 thin slices

☙ Melt the butter over low heat, add the onions and
cook until really soft, transparent and slightly crisp,
30 to 60 minutes.* Add the mustard and sprinkle with
a good pinch or two of black pepper.

☙ In a large kettle, combine the broth, bouillon cube-
water, and Chablis. Add the onions with all the
juices from their pan and keep at a very low simmer,
partially covered, for 30 to 60 minutes.**

AT THE POINT OF SERVICE

❦ Toast the French bread slices.

❦ Using large soup bowls, spoon 1 teaspoon of the applejack into each. Ladle in the soup. Float the toast on top of the soup and sprinkle each one with 2 tablespoons Parmesan.

❦ Crisscross a slice each of the Muenster and Gruyere on top.

❦ Carefully place bowls on baking sheets under hot broiler until cheese melts and bubbles.

CHEF'S NOTES

* Onions that are to be slightly crisp must be spread out across the bottom of a wide pot, not piled on top of each other. This takes a little time, so be patient. Sometimes a teaspoon of sugar will speed the process.

** Simmering means that there is slight movement and tiny little bubbles. It is not as vigorous as boiling.

"I Have Had a Dream..."

—A Midsummer Night's Dream

The women who frequented the Bedford Hamlet were stunning and svelte, clearly dressed by I. Magnin and Saks Fifth Avenue just up the street. While writing the menu, I thought of these perfectly groomed creatures, like Mrs. Kirk Douglas, Mrs. George Burns (Gracie Allen), and all the other ladies of Beverly Hills. They seemed to live on some kind of strict regime. How else could they look like that? Thus, our seven-day diet complete with calorie count was born and made the menu.

The men jumped on it, while the women splurged on fudge layer cake. Diets and fads had not taken over the country just yet, but our menu was on the cutting edge.

It was quite a block, Bedford Drive. Jax was on the corner of Wilshire and Bedford, and they did more to promote the skinny, flat-chested girl than anyone I can think of. I became one of them. Barely a size 6. It was 1960. The General Store was next door to us, selling Bonnie-and-Clyde-style haberdashery for lean ladies.

Cappriotti was the designer-owner of the General Store and she brought a look that attracted movie people, designers, and me.

Because of my proximity at the Hamlet, "Cappy" would show me everything she was doing, and invite my suggestions. This was dangerous territory for me because that burning desire to become a dress designer started again. I'd been distracted, now it was back.

In fact, many of my thoughts and ideas were translated into her collections. Theodora Von Runkle, the award-winning costume designer of *Bonnie and Clyde* fame, sketched me in many of the outfits. She used ideas and accessories from Cappy's store to dress Faye Dunaway in her role as Bonnie. These

EVEN WITH ALL OUR SUCCESS,
HARRY MADE THE LOBSTER
BISQUE EVERY MORNING AT
5:00 A.M. BEFORE ANYONE WAS
AWAKE, SO THAT IT STAYED A
FAMILY SECRET. WE WERE UP
TO ABOUT 100 GALLONS NOW
BETWEEN THE THREE STORES.
LATE IN THE AFTERNOON, WE
ALL GOT A BIKE RIDE TOGETHER.
THESE WERE SUCH HAPPY DAYS.

clothes made fashion history. The idea of becoming a dress designer with the name Cardinali was sneaking back into my mind.

I knew I could be a designer. And I knew that one day I would finally do it. I said to myself, "Get on with it...to become a dress designer is not such an impossible dream, credentials or no credentials."

GIVING BACK

We were so blessed, it didn't feel right not to give back. We wanted to share our wonderful glow in some small way. Guide Dogs for the Blind was the first group our sons were involved with, and they learned about helping others. Pets were a good way to start.

A group of us got together to form a nonprofit charity group called The Word-Of-Mouth Girls. Our goal was to provide small increments of money to various children's charities for extras. Extras like jukeboxes and music. We learned about the children from Vista Del Mar, a home for children who did not communicate with their parents for a variety of reasons, would not speak to each other, and would not communicate with their psychologists or doctors.

Music, we felt, might help, if we could raise the money to buy them a jukebox. It wasn't that hard. We're not talking about great sums of money here, and it worked magic with the kids, as if we had raised a fortune. Living in Hollywood, it was easy to get the movie stars involved. Eva Marie Saint, Cesar Romero,

"THE WORD-OF-MOUTH GIRLS:" ME, CESAR ROMERO, CAPPY, TENNER, LIZ WOLFE, AND EVA MARIE SAINT.

Richard Chamberlain, Robert Stack, Karl Malden, James Garner, Polly Bergen, and Hugh O'Brian all came to dance with the kids in our garden.

We did the same party for Maryvale, a Catholic orphanage. Even the nuns danced! The jukeboxes created a dialogue for the kids and a lesson was learned. The children were animated, lifted from their otherwise stillness.

It was like divine intervention to present this phenomenal gift to them along with a party in the garden with balloons and movie stars to dance with, because the music worked! It healed.

HUGH O'BRIAN
DANCING WITH A
LITTLE ONE.

KARL MALDEN AND
JAMES GARNER, WITH
THEIR KIDS AT THE
JUKEBOX PARTY. THIS
WAS A PARTY WHERE
YOU HAD TO EITHER
BRING YOUR OWN CHILD
OR BORROW ONE.

Photo by Edward Handler.

"MARILYN, ARE YOU SURE YOU CAN COOK?" HE ASKED

The next location came along, and it was less than a mile from Bedford Drive on a street called Beverly Drive. *The paradigm again.* It was lovingly referred to as Number Four. Number Four was very close to Bedford and everyone was concerned that we would pirate our own customers. That did happen for a while, until the customers figured out which was their favorite. With 35,000 Beverly Hills residents, plus visiting shoppers and no competition, there was enough to go around. In terms of numbers, our competition was limited to the revered Brown Derby, Chasen's, Scandia, Hillcrest Country Club, and the L.A. Country Club.

The streets rolled up early at night and that felt just fine to us. We had no valet parking, no parking lot, no bar. Beer was all we served. No wine, no liquor.

But we made a perfect hamburger.

The Beverly Drive Hamlet.

THE PERFECT HAMBURGER — YES, IT'S THE MEAT

*Y*es, *it's the bun. Yes, it's the manner of cooking: broiled, grilled, or fried. But when it comes right down to it, it's the way the meat is pattied and handled. Machine pattied—forget it. Hand pattied—it must be as if you have a hot potato in your hand, keeping the patting light and fluffy. If you handle the meat too hard or too much, the heat from your hand will coagulate the fats and toughen the whole affair. For me, I love cooking the patty in a sauté pan with a tiny bit of butter, which has been sprinkled lightly with kosher salt and cracked black pepper. Don't put the salt on the meat. Put it in the pan.*

THE BURGUNDY WINE BURGER WITH WALNUTS AND BLUE CHEESE

is wonderful. Try it. Follow the above method and at the very end, add a little Burgundy wine to the pan and let it evaporate slightly, making a delicious pan juice. Then plate up the burger on the bun, topping it with chopped walnuts, crumbled blue cheese, and a spoon or two of the pan juice over it. Or for another taste, you can make pan juice with Worcestershire sauce and a little squeeze of fresh lemon juice.

"Well, Meejum, or Rare?" was what we used to say, always with an English accent. Part of the fun was hearing the customers say "Number 7, Meejum please!" Today it's "Buy an instant meat thermometer at the grocery." Until our federal government does a better job inspecting meat, we must be certain not to eat a hamburger undercooked. The meat must be cooked to 160°, whether you like it or not.

"The Sight of Lovers
Feedeth Those in Love"

—As You Like It

Beverly Drive ("Number Four") was now open and we struck gold with Mr. Fred Brown.

He worked upstairs delivering expensive furs for Abe Lipsey, furrier to the stars. Abe Lipsey knew all the secrets and never told them or sold them. Furs  were bought and traded but to whom was never told. Fred knew those secrets too, but never waivered—his promise to Abe was secure. He never gave up so much as a clue. Fred saw an opportunity with our company and applied to Harry for a job. He accepted a busboy position as a start. From there he advanced to valet parker of all the Cadillacs and Rolls-Royces belonging to our guests. He knew everyone's name and recognized all the rich and famous people who wrapped their sun-tanned selves in furs both day and night, cool weather and warm. He spoke Spanish as well as faultless English, had a fine sense of humor, and an attitude that was all business. We made him the Manager of Number Four. A nicer, more intelligent young man was hard to find. The staff called him Mr. Brown and were proud to say it. He was twenty-two. One day he married our loveliest waitress, Gerri Chambray.

It was the first Hamlet romance. Gerri had started with us at Bedford Drive, trained by Esther Crayton and Ethel Brazil. She could have passed as a first cousin to Elizabeth Taylor. When we opened Beverly Drive, Gerri requested the counter so she could speak with her customers and get to know them. Working in the dining room didn't give you that chance, though most preferred the dining room because the tips were more generous. Not Gerri, she wanted that counter position. The counter aficionados (including radio columnist Walter Winchell) loved her straightforward personality. They wouldn't give up their counter stool for anything. Their place was reserved with Gerri.

It was one of the counter regulars who discovered that the beautiful Gerri was half Jewish. That her mother came over by boat from Austria and settled in Michigan. Very soon thereafter, her mother met a tall very handsome man of color dressed in a fine suit. They married. It was the first colored man her mother had ever seen and she fell in love with him. The customers, being mostly Jewish, loved the lore. The story intrigued them and they loved this couple. Gerri Brown still called her husband "Mr. Brown," never "Fred," for the thirty years they were at the Hamlet. There was a great deal of respect between them. After all, he was the Manager.

THE BLUES BROTHERS

With four restaurants now it was very important to have a good strong staff. My stepdad, JJ, was manager at Westwood, Mr. Brown was at Beverly Drive, Sandy Harriston was at Bedford Drive, and then we discovered Marvin. Marvin Botwin, a starling at age twenty-three. This young man was responsible, in large part, for getting us to expand, expand, expand.

Harry and Marvin together—this was serious stuff! Marvin jumped right into every department as needed and his staff respected him to such an extent that the restaurant was able to run without him. That's the sign of a *really* good Manager. (Someone who helps people develop to be as good as they can be, if not better.) The staff called him Mr. TCB (Mr. Take Care of Business). Soon he was Director of Operations—a job that was made for him. Taking note of people is how we developed our strength from within, and this strength helped us to grow. Otherwise, we didn't have a clue about how to handle expansion. It just felt right to get the best people and find a way to bring them in.

Part of Marvin's greatness was the way he loved the diversity of the staff. There was no line of demarcation between him and any staff member. He enjoyed them to the fullest extent. Each one brought something to the table. Whether it was an adage, a well-worn phrase, or a Bible lesson, he listened and respected what they had to say. Jimmy Rogers, a meticulous cook, once told him never to lock his jaw when he said anything.

When Marvin and Harry got together, they looked like the original Blues Brothers.

"You can say anything to anyone as long as you're smiling." Marvin said he never forgot it. It became part of his life's lesson, which he was happy to share.

"You have to learn to land on your feet, wherever you fall," was another lesson, as was, "Wherever a drop of rain falls, you find a wet spot." (I guess this means "step over it and move on.") And the one I love, "Today's peacock, tomorrow's feather duster" coming from the mouth of a very well paid CEO on CNN.

Now there are books and schools on good people management. But not then.

We had no manager's training program. When a manager was hired, he had to feel his way and learn by mistakes. And one would *hope to God*, get it right. Since it was important to know how to do everyone's job, we began placing management hopefuls into each department to learn. This was the right move. Everyone who leads must know how to play every instrument in the band. We were very fortunate to attract some very good people. And some bad ones—one of the new Managers would drink his coffee with about three ounces of bourbon in it. It was not always easy to discover those little secrets.

While I was cooking and practicing, Marvin was thinking big and looking for locations. He wanted to talk to big developers, try to persuade them to put us in to their new buildings. *I did not care for this at all.* It seemed to depersonalize everything we had created. To suddenly become a part of a lunchtime feeding frenzy for scores and scores of high-rise employees was not in my orbit. Harry, who had become a real businessman, was not as romantic as I tended to be. He thought highly of this new method for expansion. So Tishman became Number Five, downtown. The décor was like a woodsy, tartan-plaid pub. Once that was finished, I felt my job was completed and I left it to the "Blues Brothers" to run everything. *This was a turning point in the Hamlets. It was no longer the treasured neighborhood secret, everyone's love story. It was a chain.*

Except for the "21" Club in New York and Dave Chasen, who had started with a hamburger and a bowl of chili too, we were the rabbit leading the pack.

You'd look around and there was no one behind us. We were out there for fifteen years before the imitators and the spin-offs came into view. We set the trend for the whole industry.

Then, the "H's" started to call. It seemed like every company that started with an H wanted to acquire us. H. J. Heinz, Hilton Hotels, and Holiday Inns. Now the offers were up to $3 million. *This was better than Charlie Feldman's $250,000.* It was certainly interesting to know how much we were worth on the street, but we couldn't be budged. It wasn't even tempting. It was ours. We had worked too bloody hard (and were insanely jealous over our reputation) to be taken over by a conglomerate and mutate into something unrecognizable.

"ALL THE WORLD'S A STAGE"

—As You Like It

Quietly enjoying our success, we moved our home from the 500 block on Bedford Drive to the 700 block on Linden Drive, in Beverly Hills, but couldn't yet afford to furnish it. So our voices boomeranged all across the old heavy walls and resonated up and across the glorious two-story-high ceilings for a long time.

This went on for two years, until I learned that the Fox West Coast Theater in San Francisco was being razed. I got there just before the heavy ball crushed everything to smithereens. This theater had been built during the American Depression, while there were soup lines and yet here was a magnificent powder room all decorated with eighteen-karat gold detail. The furniture in the lobby was fit for emperors or kings. I bought the room and a few pieces of baronial furniture for very little and sent it home. It worked handsomely, but our house smelled like salted popcorn for a very long time.

Opening a Hamlet downtown evidently made us too visible to the big guys. One day we got a letter from the Governor Jerry Brown. (Pat Brown's son, some

Our popcorn living room.

Fox West Powder Room.

"MARILYN, ARE YOU SURE YOU CAN COOK?" HE ASKED

said, was politically extremely left of liberal.) He informed us that we were practicing reverse discrimination and mandated that we "mix up the palette!" This was a blow. A blow because many of our employees had been unemployed and on welfare, and now because of their fine performances, were gainfully employed, paying taxes, and saving money to send their children to college. And we were told to shake things up because we were practicing "reverse discrimination"! (The staff didn't like the letter and neither did we.) What would happen to Martha Graham's dance group? Did the Rockettes in New York City get a similar letter? We were going to appeal, but in the end one concept is as bad as the other. So we decided to let nature take its course. If it worked well, fine. If it didn't, we would have another of life's hard lessons to try to make people get along with each other under the rule of law. *Our government in action.*

THE WATTS RIOT

1965. Watts exploded. It changed our lives dramatically. We had a big group of wonderful people depending on us just as we depended on them. Full of love and professionalism in just the right measure, and overnight they became disenfranchised. These were people who had no forum in which to speak or be heard. It was painful. Their need to love and trust in someone or something was palpable.

So they came to us. We heard all their gripes about the job, about money, debt, health, love affairs, spousal abuse, and children. Our hearts were there for them in every instance. *I was the one with all the breasts, like the wolf in Roman mythology. With the biological ability to feed everyone but myself. The nurturer.* We had always cared for our staff, but now something very big was happening. Something very different.

The night it actually started, Marvin (Mr. Take Care of Business) had to see what was really going on. To see if it was possible to keep things moving and keep people safe. He hid on the floor in the back of an old Pontiac with a blanket over him while a few of the cooks drove him through the area. They told him when he could look up. This was dangerous stuff!

The employees could not get to work, so Marvin arranged to have several employees drive into the riot zone. Marvin and William (whom we trusted with our lives) rented a three-ton truck, closed on the sides but open on the top, big enough to hold fifty people. He would pick up the staff who lived in Watts and bring them in safely. Getting home was another war story. Some had to be put up in motels outside Watts, near the Hamlets where they worked. Others were driven back, hiding on the floor, through the fires in their neighborhoods. They just simply could not get home, and they were frightened.

Everyone tried to hide their fear and do their jobs. We stayed open and staffed. Our compassion toward our staff's needs was at such a high pitch that we had little left over for each other. *It must be a common feeling among psychologists, psychiatrists, and social workers, particularly during times of crisis. You live outside of yourself, until you look into your own soul and find that the depths of your lock-up has no key!*

Eventually, the lines of communication and unique closeness we felt began to show signs of strain. You could feel the quiet. Here was a people so completely confused that they didn't know who to hear or what to feel any more. It would have been dangerous for any of us to shift to a particular political "side"—there was definitely the element of danger as far as we were concerned, and yet the fight had reason and roots.

Overnight, blacks were against blacks, blacks were against whites, whites were against blacks, and whites were against whites.

After the Watts riots, many things changed. We received threatening phone calls warning that a bomb would explode in one of our restaurants or in our home if we continued to employ so many blacks. We had some very heavy decisions to make. Should we close the stores until this blew over? Would it blow over? *Where can we run to keep our children safe? Would our customers be confused as well? Would we have a business left, after all these fifteen years?* We packed up the family and moved quickly to the Beverly Wilshire Hotel. The hotel suggested we use only the freight elevator for security reasons. Harry and I made the decision to stay open in all the stores and follow the curfew hours so the employees could get home safely.

We got on the phone and made 450 phone calls to each and every one of our people to tell them of our decision and comfort them. It took over twelve hours to make these calls, but the staff were so happy to hear from us.

Most everyone said they would come to work, except one man, a pantry man, who said he was too confused and didn't know if he should work for white people. There were no bombs, but can you imagine what it might have been, had we made the wrong call?

We lived in such fear. There were meetings after meetings in each of the stores to lift the morale of the staff so they wouldn't be conflicted.

A PERSPECTIVE

Watts occupies about two and one-half square miles. There is no real consensus on its boundaries, but for our purposes, let us say 92nd street on the north, Alameda Street on the east, Imperial Avenue on the south, and Central Avenue on the west. The McCone Commission estimate on total Negro population was 432,900 with the number active in the riot at 40,260 (about 15% of the adult population).

A tour of these backstreets reveals the unmistakable blight and deterioration of a typical slum: littered streets, yards, and alleys; unpainted, rundown houses and shabby business sections; scattered dumps and trash heaps, and a general appearance of neglect. Ugliness abounds in such eyesores as a mountain of used tires on the fringe of a residential district, and a block-long, two-story high scrap metal heap adjacent to the Jordan Downs housing project.

Unemployment at the time was over 13%; more than 10,000 families were headed by females; these families included more that 10,000 children under eighteen. About 35% of these children were not living with both parents. Even if employed, families still only earned less than $3,000 per year. Could there be any wonder that a Watts riot occurred?

How could it not?

We tried to help them sort things out a little more easily. I remember telling them that maybe this horrible event would turn out to be a positive one, after all. That they might now be heard as a voice. Everyone needs to be heard. The American people were good, I told them they would see. *I hoped I was right.*

Times were definitely changing. From the mid-'50s through the mid-'60s, Steve Allen and Jack Paar opened more intelligent pathways for blacks on TV, in satire, and theatrical opportunities. Tony Brown was a very sophisticated moderator who appeared weekly on PBS in a thirty-minute Emmy-winning television newsmagazine called *Tony Brown's Journal.* The show dealt with issues for and about blacks. *Soul Train* was a '60s dance show featuring R&B produced and hosted by Don Cornelius, and it engendered a lot of musical pride. Of course, in the '70s open forums for the alternative were seen in combative shows hosted by Joe Pine and Wally George. These shows offered a screaming declaration to the First Amendment. They were generally viewed as opinionated hate mongers, serving

HILDA JAMES, DEBRA TAYLOR, CATHY MORRISON, ESTHER CRAYTON, LIL GORDON, MAL PRUETT, PEGGY, CECILA "CW" (SEATED), JIM ROGERS (OF STUFFED BELL PEPPERS FAME), MONROE WINSTON, DAVID BACON, HILDA ROCCA, BOB BELLE, AND REESE (THE BARTENDER).

the white racists. They were the first of the Jerry Springer-type shows. The more hell that broke loose, the higher the ratings. At least people were being heard. The silent '50s were dead.

The withdrawal was a problem for me, after Watts. There was business as usual but you could feel the silence. They were afraid to take sides. The calls from waitresses who wanted to share their personal or business-related problems with us just stopped. Nurturing others was such a part of me—without it, I couldn't center. It seemed like I was nothing but an answering machine, spitting out solutions for the problems du jour. Nothing more. *It was only the confusion of a people denied the right to predict their own future?*

It had become all about business, nothing but on-the-run problem solving. Work with no soul. I had helped a lot of people along the way realize their dreams, and maybe it was time for my dreams now.

I had raised two boys and a successful business. If I may be allowed to think of business as a masculine pursuit, I had lived in a man's world. I began to long for something soft and feminine. Having a daughter I'm sure would have helped.

I needed something more feminine to think about—something pretty, like dresses and fabrics and colors. *Maybe Cardinali the fashion designer could finally be born.* Being the mom of two little boys and working in the business so closely with my husband made me long to create something of my own. I needed to feel the female side of myself. Because I had lost the sweet closeness with the girls and the waitress classes, I felt empty. I struggled with this. They had the Civil Rights Act now, thank goodness. It gave them a forum, a face. Maybe it was my time now. *Because of Watts, Cardinali was born.*

"It is astonishing to encounter a slim, Camille-like little woman who has the tenacity of a tiger and who thinks like a man. But that is Marilyn Lewis, who, with her husband, has built Hamburger Hamlets into a fantastic operation. When I say that Marilyn thinks like a man, I mean that the décor of most of the Hamburger Hamlets is masculine—oak paneling and that sort of thing."
—Roundabout, Los Angeles Times, March 8, 1964

Harry thought it would be all right as long as the family and our growing business came first. *In that order*. But first, we had to face a closing. The original little Hamlet had to close. It was an eighteen-year run.

The other Hamlets were new business models now. They were more linear, more sophisticated, and ran as smooth as a Rolls-Royce engine. Mr. TCB was out there looking for more locations. Joe Lordon was hiring more and more staff. Vern Boyce (with us from the beginning of Westwood in 1955) was now director of operations (and were his hands ever full). Stella Nelson was purchasing as fast as she could, and I was thinking of the menu nonstop. Mr. Metz was worrying more and more, and George Kay was making sure the health department liked us. It was a full-blown staff. Those charming years in the first little place on Sunset had passed. And as it turned out, the culture had changed. Whisky a Go Go had just opened on the opposite corner and was attracting long lines of hippies, all spaced out on drugs and all over the sidewalks, leaving no access for customers. You couldn't even see the entrance to the Hamlet or those little screen doors. The dream and the charm were over. The '60s were hard upon us.

Maybe everything has to die....

"Then Hamlet gets hers stuck in the shoulder,

An' sees how he's framed from the start,

So he switches the swords on Laertes,

An' he stabs the poor bum through the heart.

Then he runs his sword right through his uncle,

An' he says 'Well, let's call it a day.'

Then the Queen dies, the King dies, an' Ham dies,

I calls it a helluva play!" —*Author unknown*

And I call it a helluva run!

Eighteen years. We did nothing to help us cry. *Our original Hamlet no longer there. But we had to buck up, stifle our tears, and move on. I look back and think we should have sat down and had a good cry, and a good hug. Even a glass of bubbly would have been a celebration and an acknowledgment of what was happening, how things were changing. But no, it was "Business!"*

BOHEMIA DIES OF SUCCESS

Of course, we still had to have a Hamlet on Sunset, so we moved four blocks
west, to the foot of Truesdale, a wealthy enclave north of the Strip. It was a huge
space and required some bold design. *Very different from the original one everyone
had loved.* I patterned its interior and comfort level on the high-priced places the
neighbors liked to frequent: Scandia, Chasen's, the Windsor, and their country

Harry was a private in the Air Transport Command in 1941, and was destined for Karachi, India. That is, until Irving "Swifty" Lazar intervened. Instead, Irving requested that Harry be shipped to Special Services in New York, to audition for Moss Hart's air force musical Winged Victory, *which was set to open on Broadway for a limited engagement. George Cukor was directing, and starring were Mario Lanza, Karl Malden, Red Buttons, Lee J. Cobb, Martin Ritt, Edmond O'Brien, and Don Taylor. Music was by David Rose (of* Stripper *fame). What a close call that was! The troops were boarding the trucks, just as Harry was called away.*

I may never have met him!

clubs. Red leather, high-backed wing chairs, the by-now-standard book-matched walnut paneling, the sunflower carpeting, tufted booths, and valet parking. This time there was a big bar. Our home went on the block again at the bank. It was very risky but very successful in the end.

Imagine such a setting for a hamburger, a martini, and lobster bisque. Such a place with such a name sitting at the foot of Hollywood's gods and goddesses. Truesdale. Irving (Swifty) and Mary Lazar lived there.

When I learned that Swifty was responsible for Harry not being shipped off to India in 1941, I felt compelled to send him a letter thanking him for saving Harry's life. In my letter, I told Irving (the name he preferred) that he would be our guest at the Hamlet on Sunset forever. We placed a gold star above his favorite booth, which is still there. When he got my letter, he called to say, "That's just great, honey! I'll bring Cary Grant in every Sunday—now he'll really owe me!"

SWIFTY AND MARY LAZAR,
TITA (MRS. SAMMY) CAHN,
AND TONY BENNETT SITTING
ON THE STAIRS WITH HARRY
AT ONE OF OUR PARTIES.
THEY TOOK THE BEST SEATS
IN THE HOUSE.

Swifty was a powerful agent in Hollywood, and he did bring Cary Grant in, many times. Bogart gave him the nickname because of the instantaneous, incredible deals he made for his clients. In fact, when I told him I was thinking of writing a book, I asked him how long it should be. He said "Kid, when you're ready, give it to me. I'll just weigh it in my hands, and tell you when you're finished."

Moving to the big new place created a flurry of mixed opinions. Some of the more affluent new customers absolutely loved it, because it was big, plush, and comfortable. They could roll down the hill and go to "their place" without a lot of driving. A kind of reverse snobbism became apparent. For people so enormous in stature and power as

GIG YOUNG AND HARRY LEWIS
READY TO BE SHIPPED OUT.

Lew Wasserman and the David Wolpers to entertain at a place called Hamburger Hamlet was fun for them. Dean Martin had his seat at the bar every Sunday night. You'd look around some nights and everyone you'd ever read about was in that place. Just being comfortable. The Kirk Douglases, the Aaron Spellings. These were the emperors!

But to the wonderful "crazies" who had driven us nuts late, late at night during our humble beginnings, we had done something terrible. We were no longer this "wonderful, hardworking couple." We had gone "big" on them, sold out. Whenever Edward G. Robinson saw us, he'd say to Harry in his gangster voice "You sold out—you went straight on us, Toots." I tried to understand their feelings. Now these guys are all grown up with their own children and they actually "tear up" when they remember those days. Even Warren Beatty recently told us that he was an early "Hamlet baby," and spent "many a night in those booths." But, wouldn't reveal his "good" stories, he just smiled and held onto his privacy. Everyone has a story.

We haven't owned the Hamlets since 1987 and still the stories go on. Francis Davis (once married to the fabulous Miles Davis) keeps the old Sunset Hamlet stories rolling.

Aaron Spelling
Chairman Of The Board
Chief Executive Officer

July 30, 1997

Dear Marilyn,

You have to understand that when I first went to the Hamlet, I was so poor that I considered it to be like Chasen's!

A lot of actors made it their hangout, and going there made me feel like I was part of Hollywood! My favorite thing was the cheddar cheese and bacon with Russian dressing. I wanted all I could get for the little money I had!

Love,

Aaron

Aaron Spelling

P.S.   Candy also sends her love.

As:lb

Norman R. Brokaw
Chairman of the Board

September 19, 1997

Dear Marilyn and Harry:

What fond memories I have of our 50 plus years of friendship. It's so nice to look back and think that we were all together at the very beginning of our careers.

I remember so well, when I was the first mailboy and messenger in the legendary William Morris mailroom. It was always on Thursday that I would go to Paramount, RKO and then Warner Bros. to get in line to pick up the clients' checks. The line was often long and every now and then one could see Jack Warner walking in the background and the likes of Jerry Wald, Mike Curtiz, and Solly Biano.

But, I always noticed that Harry was always the first in line ahead of Peter Lorre, Sydney Greenstreet, and a few of the young starlets under contract to the studio. Harry, you were such a good, young actor, no wonder Warner Bros. had you under contract.

Your friend,
Norman R. Brokaw

Hamburgers
to Hemlines

ROBERT W. RICHARDS

PART TWO

Cardinali Is Born

"Hamburgers to Hemlines Intertwined." The press had a field day with those words. I wasn't amused then, but it was prophetic. There were indeed similarities between the two businesses. Even the stock market claimed that when hemlines went up, stocks followed; when hemlines came down, stocks dropped.

In the design business, buyers learn quickly not to show a single emotion while viewing a collection. Poker face was de rigeur. *That tore me up*. To get a written order became the very center of my being. In a room full of hungry people, you can tell if they're pleased. They eat, they drink, they converse, and they make "all gone." They even tell you how much they enjoyed it.

So where was the nexus between these two very diverse businesses?

Maybe in the words: What's hot? What's not? Perfect words for food *and* fashion. *The press are the only ones having a good time here.*

My brand-new factory was set up on the edge of Beverly Hills, right next door to the Wonder Bread Bakery. The smell of sweet yeasty dough made me hungry all the time. Not exactly a good feeling when you're designing and fitting small, narrow clothes. I got used to it after awhile, but it always made me ravenous. All I could think about was a fried baloney sandwich on Wonder Bread with a lot of catsup. *The habit of thinking about food at all times never left me. My two sensual gifts. Clothes and food.*

The cost of starting a design business goes like this: First, you have to buy all your fabrics. You can't buy little pieces, you have to buy a whole bolt and pay C.O.D. or use a letter of credit from the bank. To guess what you're going to need out of that bolt can be as mind-boggling as figuring out how many cheese blintzes you need for the day, only more expensive. Most trained designers start with a sketch, then cut a muslin shell, and only then cut into the precious fabric. I started by draping the fabric while it was still on the bolt, then cut directly into the fabric. No muslin for me. Very costly strategy, but being untrained, I couldn't "hear" the fabric any other way. It was a very risky business *just like the restaurant business.* The public either nods, or it doesn't.

Hiring a pattern maker is like hiring a chef. I got a good one. He was Greek, named Chris. He followed me perfectly and cut it brilliantly. *I couldn't have normal up-and-down seams, I had to have asymmetrical ones.* Truly, it was as if a design angel was standing near me and giving me these wonderful ideas. Whatever it was, the ideas were good and the clothes were beautiful. I'm grateful to my angel.

And here, the relationship between hamburgers and hemlines ends. Getting your money back is another story. The stores take their discounts. Payments are ninety days after delivery. You need a money tree in the design business to give you that bridge funding. In the food business stands a cash cow.

Jim Meisner, the merchandise manager at Saks Fifth Avenue on the West Coast, loved what I showed him. He promptly called New York. Mr. Meisner could not wait to show me off to New York. As in "Look what I've discovered!" The protocol was all new to me. Generally, talent originated in New York, not in California. Mr. Meisner was thrilled at his discovery, but nervous about New York. He was fairly confident that the "home office" would love the collection as much as he did.

In the meantime, Tenner had moved to London with her husband and was busy raising four children. We wrote back and forth. She was genuinely happy for me, that I was finally living my life's dream: being Cardinali, the designer.

Then one night she appeared at my door in Beverly Hills with her children in hand, needing a place to stay and some employment. Her true-blue husband had become a little too fond of his secretary. Ruth fled with the children back to the States. I had no warning at all of this. In fact, her letters were in complete denial, raving about what a wonderful place London was to raise children, and all about the different customs. "They do eat so properly," she would tell me. *It seemed her husband had emptied their bank account, after all those years of marriage.*

There was not a moment of hesitation on my part. She was going to be my new assistant in Cardinali, travel with me, and be my sales rep. After all, this was Tenner. My lifelong best friend. My big sister.

In New York, the fashion world is different. They tend to look down their noses at "dress designers" unless they are out of New York. And yet some of the greatest designers of that times were the avant-garde Rudi Gernreich, the elegant James Galanos, and Jean-Louis, designer for the stars. All from California. Not to mention the studio designers like Edith Head, Walter Plunkett, and Adrian. But they didn't count in terms of retail. New York was busy creating huge careers for Donald Brooks, Bill Blass, Norrell, and Pauline Trigere. Not a lot of women. In general, men owned the slot.

I arrived at the Plaza Hotel, where everyone showed their collections, and was humbled by the price tag per day for the suite. You had to have a proper living room to show the collection. You had to have a bedroom and you had to put the models up as well. A dresser was required (that would be Tenner) and a hairdresser who also helped book appointments with the buyers. Hugh York was our hairdresser and he was constantly "looking around" the city at night. I'd be so worried, I'd call every hospital and the police to announce him missing, until I realized he was just out on the town. There were fourteen black fiberglass wardrobe cases, customized to hold the collection flat without wrinkles. Setting up the shows in New York was like a circus. All that was missing were the parrots and pets. Harry was not amused.

In Los Angeles I had had only one press showing.

The *Los Angeles Times*, my hometown paper, was very good to me. Fay Hammond wrote rave reviews, as did Jody Jacobs of *Women's Wear Daily*. This gave me stamina.

Being a woman in the rag business was tough. I wasn't getting the callbacks I wanted, or the appointments. It was very expensive to sit and wait in New York. Had I left a man's name, I probably would have had my dance card

Illustration by Robert Richards.

My hot pants were really hot! The long brown and white English plaid boucle coat covered tiny little matching hot pants, with a wide brown suede belt hung asymmetrically from leather belt loops.

Illustration by Robert Richards.

"MARILYN, ARE YOU SURE YOU CAN COOK?" HE ASKED

filled. It's just the way the game was played. The male designers knew how to treat the buyers and have silly fun with them. I just didn't have that nature. I was quieter, and still learning how to live my role as Cardinali. *Slightly elegant and naturally a bit shy by nature. But my shyness was like a "front" for a lot of nerves and courage.*

Everyone hung out at Elaine's or Andy Warhol's Factory, after hours, while I soaked in the ultra-long Plaza bathtub, worrying about the buyers and having stage fright. Occasionally, I'd order up a leg of lamb and roast it in our little Plaza kitchen. Everyone was so pleased that our suite smelled deliciously fragrant with garlic and rosemary and the buyers ate it up! I won them over a little bit with my cooking. Perhaps it made me more human to them.

Illustration by Robert Richards.

"The West Coast is dismissed by the East Coast, which is really a shame, because the Midwest falls in between and is dismissed by both." —M.L.

ROAST LEG OF LAMB CARDINALI

We sliced this paper-thin and served it on thinly sliced baguettes with a drop of chutney and Dijon. Oh, and of course, a glass of champagne. The buyers loved it.

Read the recipe through so you will understand the special potato treatment.

I personally love mint jelly with lamb, but you may also make a simple gravy: skim the fat from the pan drippings and pour the juices into a saucepan. Add a cup of dry white wine and boil until reduced by half. Taste for seasonings and drizzle over the lamb.

- ☙ SECURE A 5- TO 7-POUND, BONELESS LEG OF LAMB. BRING TO ROOM TEMPERATURE. PREHEAT THE OVEN TO 400°.
- ☙ CHECK WEIGHT OF THE LAMB ON THE BATHROOM SCALE AND MAKE A NOTE OF IT.
- ☙ WASH LAMB AND DRY WITH PAPER TOWELS. RUB LAMB ALL OVER WITH OLIVE OIL. USING A SMALL POINTY KNIFE OR A METAL SKEWER, MAKE GASHES ALL AROUND LAMB, EVERY INCH OR SO.
- ☙ RUB THE FOLLOWING MIXTURE INTO THE GASHES:
  4 CLOVES GARLIC, PEELED AND CUT IN SLIVERS
  2 TABLESPOONS DRIED ROSEMARY, RUBBED BETWEEN YOUR FINGERS TO RELEASE THE OILS
- ☙ SPRINKLE THE LAMB EVENLY WITH 1 TABLESPOON KOSHER SALT AND A FEW COARSE GRINDINGS OF BLACK PEPPER.

continued   Roast Leg of Lamb Cardinali

❦ PLACE AN 8 X 8-INCH OR SIMILAR-SIZED CASSEROLE CONTAINING $^1/_2$ CUP OF WATER ON THE BOTTOM RACK OF THE OVEN (YOU WILL USE THIS FOR THE POTATOES AND MEANWHILE IT WILL CATCH THE DRIPPINGS). PLACE THE LAMB DIRECTLY ONTO THE CENTER OVEN RACK, ABOVE THE CASSEROLE. ROAST THE LAMB FOR APPROXIMATELY 25 MINUTES PER POUND FOR MEDIUM RARE.

❦ ONE HOUR BEFORE LAMB IS READY: PEEL AND SLICE THINLY, USING A MANDOLIN IF YOU HAVE ONE:

3 POUNDS RUSSET POTATOES

❦ REMOVE THE CASSEROLE FROM THE HOT OVEN AND BRUSH THE DRIPPINGS EVENLY OVER THE SURFACE SO THE POTATOES WON'T STICK. QUICKLY OVERLAP HALF OF THE SLICES IN ONE LAYER. SPRINKLE WITH KOSHER SALT AND PEPPER, AND DOT WITH A LITTLE BUTTER (2 TO 3 TABLESPOONS SWEET BUTTER, IN TOTAL). BUILD ANOTHER LAYER IN THE SAME WAY AND RETURN TO THE OVEN UNDERNEATH THE LAMB.

❦ WHEN THE LAMB IS DONE (140°-145° FOR MEDIUM RARE), REMOVE FROM OVEN AND ALLOW TO REST FOR AT LEAST 10 MINUTES BEFORE SLICING. THE POTATOES WILL BE BUBBLY AND CRISP, AND GOLDEN BROWN.

❦ IN A SMALL SAUCEPAN, HEAT GENTLY:

1 SMALL CAN STEWED TOMATOES, WELL DRAINED

❦ SPOON OVER THE POTATOES AND SERVE.

"I Have Set
My Life Upon a Cast"

—Richard III

Finally, Saks arranged for my one big meeting with all the head buyers in the country. I had a thirty-five-piece collection of suits, dresses, and gowns, and only one appointment on the books. *What if they don't like it? What if they don't make a buy? I was having the flop-sweats.*

The Saks contingency of buyers were lined up like a row of ducks. We were first on their agenda, to see a new collection by "this California designer." It was 7:00 A.M., an ungodly hour to get everything ready with models, hairdresser, and the dresser, who snapped, buttoned, and put everything in place. But that was my punishment for being from California.

Harry, thank God, was there, so I didn't have to feel so alone in the big city. In fact, he was asleep in the bedroom when they all started arriving, one by one. They entered the dark bedroom and threw their coats on top of him. Not wanting to embarrass anyone, he didn't move.

Mr. Meisner was in the living room, as nervous as he could be. It was very important to him that New York like me, so he could make a large buy. The buyers didn't show an ounce of emotion until the very end, when they burst into applause. Mr. Meisner got so excited he ran into the bedroom where Harry was trying to sleep again, pulled back the covers screaming, "Oh, my God, I think I'm going to have a baby! They loved it!" He dropped the covers over Harry's head and darted out. They wrote a sizable order for the whole country and I knew I was in business.

Since my one and only appointment with Saks had paid off, I didn't think it smart to hang around waiting for no one to call. So we all packed up and went back home to fill this amazing first order. Now let me tell you, that took a pack of people. Drapers, finishers, and sample makers who had to be paid every week.

Talented people whose hands sewed with little stitches and flew like butterflies. Packing up their finished work was like wrapping delicate pieces of Dresden china. Even the packaging was done with such care. Once the orders were delivered, I held my breath and waited. Meanwhile, at Saks in L.A. Gail Hensley, the Los Angeles couture buyer, fashion director Liz Brady, and Jim Meisner did everything to promote me.

Gail would tell me, "Marilyn, they're flying out the door. We don't even have time to unpack them and they're sold!"

"THE GLASS OF FASHION AND THE MOLD OF FORM"

—Hamlet

Illustration by Robert Richards.

The black and white woven bouclé suits had white satin linings and blouses with jeweled buttons, perfect for lunch. Jeweled buttons were never worn in the daytime, and certainly never mixed on tweed at that time. Betsy Bloomingdale bought this very suit to wear at lunch, as did Mrs. Crown in New York, Mrs. Robert Fluor, and Mrs. Montgomery Fisher.

My color palette was interesting. Mustard and royal blue tweeds were mixed with soft mustard and burgundy print chiffon linings. The collection was shown with nude stockings and a red suede pump. Tweeds came from France, laces from Switzerland, and silks from Italy.

Cleveland, I Was Seven Years Old....

Mother had a better job now, at the Baily Company. We'd stand in line to get her paycheck. Only it wasn't a paycheck, it was a spare amount of cash with some coins and it was paid to her in a little brown manila envelope. Funny about things you never forget. Like when Mother and I went to buy shoes for school. It broke my heart when I saw her open the little brown envelope to pay for my shoes. It stayed indelibly inscribed on my heart, her doing that. Now, when there were so many red shoes.

For Cardinali, red suede was my neutral shoe, no matter what color the outfit. Another year, my neutral shoe was shell-pink suede. Paprika douvet cloth made up a long-skirted theater suit with a burgundy velvet collar. The slit in the skirt showed off a naughty leg and finished with an innocent white crepe satin shirt with organdy butterflies sewn intricately into the bodice. (I've always said that when a woman sits down, we should still see something interesting.) The details were exquisite, and the finished garment looked like it was made in Paris with its ample handstitched seams, one could practically wear them inside out. Everyone said it gave them such pleasure to see the painstaking workmanship on the underside of each of my garments. I once sent out a model wearing the dress inside out. It was amazingly funny. Picture the faces of the buyers, until they got it!

Having a fine bench tailor was unusual for a woman's line. Bench tailors were generally employed to mold a perfect shoulder in men's suits. The Cardinali suits were all handworked and steamed like an expensive man's suit. They required the hands of a fine tailor and lots of seamstresses, whose fingers moved like lightning bugs.

Name Dropping

The Hollywood crowd was beginning to wear Cardinali. It may sound like name dropping, but the "who," as in who is wearing your clothes, was the ticket. The famous and the wives and girlfriends of the famous were strong supporters. Dionne Warwick wore Cardinali on her album covers, Eydie Gorme, on the stage. The collectors were, fortunately, collecting: Nancy Reagan (she could stand for hours like royalty during fittings), Betsy Bloomingdale (stunning), Mrs. Aaron Spelling (doll-like), Polly Bergen (soft and feminine around fashion), Mrs. Louis Jourdan, Mrs. Kirk Douglas (elegant taste), Mrs. Walter Matthau (Carol—so in love with Walter). Alexis Smith, Rhonda Fleming, Candace Bergen, and her beautiful mother, Frances Bergen, Nancy Sinatra, Sr., and both of her beautiful daughters, Nancy and Tina, Mrs. Crown of New York's Crown Towers, Barbara Walters (so petite), Mrs. Robert Fluor of the Fluor Corporation, Mrs. Gordon Getty, and a host of Texans. Other names, to whom I'm so grateful: Leonore (Mrs. Walter) Annenberg (a fascinating woman), Ginny Mancini, Mrs. Conrad Hilton, Jr., Mrs. Henry Fonda, Judy Flowers, Mary Jones Marshall, Jody Jacobs, Carole Kay, Phyllis Tabach, Paula Kent Meehan, Geri Brawerman, Jean Habelson, Tita Cahn, Ruth Roman, Greer Garson, Mrs. Hal David, Mrs. Hoffert Dailey, Mrs. Gwynne Robinson, Rubye Beattie, Joni Smith, Margo Hirsh, Julie Hutner, Helene Tobias, Betty Resnick, Mrs. Thomas A. Sullivan of San Francisco, and Mrs. Henry Cruger Van Schaack, Jr., of Denver.

Illustration by Robert Richards.

"MARILYN, ARE YOU SURE YOU CAN COOK?" HE ASKED

Endorsements Are
Life's Blood for a Designer

Perfume, bed wear, neckties, scarves, pajamas, panties, bras, hosiery, lingerie, and men's wear—i.e., accessories. In fashion, this was where the money was (and is). The AIDS virus was killing off the most creative male designers. Investors were beginning to study the field for women. There were very few. Donna Karan was probably still at design school when Charlie Revson of Revlon, and his then wife Lynn invited Harry and me to their Fifth Avenue apartment in New York to discuss a Cardinali perfume. But first, an intimate dinner in their library, followed by a tour of Lynn Revson's dressing room. She was so proud of it, and it was thrilling for me to see such order. *Everything I loved. Beautiful clothes and accessories and everything in place.* After dinner, instead of a business discussion, it was off to Doubles, a super-private disco under the Sherry Netherland Hotel, to dance the night away. There was no concrete discussion about anything concerning Cardinali "parfum" or endorsements. I surmised that this was the way one did business in this industry—first you see whether you like each other and have fun together. Essential components for a partnership of harmony.

So, I waited. Harry would spend weekends with me, flying in from the West Coast to bail me out anyway he could.

Illustrations by Robert Richards.

If I had a problem getting a certain female buyer from Bonwit Teller to respond to my calls, he'd suit up and pay her a visit. Arm in arm, they would return to the Plaza and have the greatest time together while I showed the collection. *Because of Harry, Cardinali was eventually written into Bonwit Teller, then to Bergdorf Goodman.*

Charlie Revson was a health food fanatic, and he showed his affection by sending Harry some utterly flavorless natural peanut butter, and some fake eggs he had his lab cook up. The next thing I knew, he died. Charlie was gone and so was my endorsement. *Stomach-ache time.*

A Saks buyer from Chevy Chase, Maryland, was viewing one of my collections at the Plaza Hotel in New York, and she told me about an empty site in Washington, D.C., right next door to a very posh Elizabeth Arden. She thought it would be a perfect new location for a Hamlet and suggested we call the developer. *Hamburgers and hemlines really are intertwined!* "You never know," she said, "He might just want to build a restaurant for you."

A QUANTUM LEAP

We had never wanted to venture out of California and the thought of Chevy Chase was a quantum leap. But one night in New York it hit me: Why not? We had already protected our trademark, our name, by flying individual bags of salted potato chips from Los Angeles to Washington via the major carriers. Whatever it took. And having a business on the East Coast would help "lionize" our impact.

As long as I was showing in New York twice a year, why not build another little fiefdom on the East Coast? It certainly was a challenge, and I did seem to like a challenge. It would give me a saner sense of purpose than Cardinali, and it would be good to expand our presence into this market on both fronts, I reasoned with myself persuasively.

Harry flew out to meet me and we took the New York shuttle to D.C. *A fun trip, only one hour, easy.* The landlord, Flo Orisman (a man), had visited the Hamlets on the West Coast many times and loved them, that much was encouraging. Best of all, there was nothing at all like them in D.C. at the time.

The space was right. The parking was good and the sign privileges generous. We entered into the usual twenty five year lease. Sherrod Marshall, our architect, spent hours on the phone with me in development. Richard Nixon was in the White House.

I felt the décor for the Chevy Chase Hamlet should be like a beautiful walnut-paneled library in an affluent home. The first restaurant of its kind serving the lowly hamburger (but not so lowly when I got done with it). As always, we took the high road with everything, befitting all the senators and congressmen who came to see America's favorite dish elevated to a new height.

We had more devotees of the Hamlet in Washington than we had expected. Kids who had gone to UCLA or USC were now raising their own families on the East Coast, in our Hamlets. The world was growing smaller. We were now up to eighteen restaurants and I was spending more time in the air than I had figured on. One suitcase was always packed.

ZUCCHINI ZIRCLES WITH
SECRET APRICOT SAUCE

SERVES 6

Yep, that was the name. It was all in fun and a lot of grown-ups out there still said it as they were growing up—"Zucchini Zircles please"—and no one ever asked why.

- ❧ SCRUB WITH A BRUSH, BUT DO NOT PEEL, 3 SMALL ZUCCHINIS. CUT THEM IN "ZIRCLES" LIKE POKER CHIPS, ABOUT DOUBLE THE THICKNESS OF A SILVER DOLLAR. PLACE ON A PAPER-TOWEL-LINED BAKING SHEET.

- ❧ HEAT A GENEROUS AMOUNT OF OIL (AT LEAST 2 INCHES DEEP) IN A DEEP FAT FRYER TO 375°.

- ❧ SET OUT THREE SHALLOW PLATES AND FILL ONE WITH 3/4 CUP MILK, THE SECOND WITH 1/2 CUP FLOUR, AND THE THIRD WITH 1 CUP SEASONED DRY ITALIAN BREADCRUMBS.

- ❧ DIP THE ZIRCLES FIRST INTO THE FLOUR, THEN INTO THE MILK, THEN INTO THE BREADCRUMBS, AND NOW PLACE THEM ON A WIRE RACK.

- ❧ USING TONGS, FRY A FEW ZIRCLES AT A TIME, UNTIL GOLDEN (ABOUT 20 TO 30 SECONDS), AND DRAIN ON PAPER TOWELS.

- ❧ SPRINKLE THE ZIRCLES WITH A LITTLE POWDERED SUGAR, AND SERVE WITH SECRET APRICOT SAUCE FOR DIPPING. *Today everyone wants their own dip to dip into. Little ramekins set on a long rectangular dish (Asian style) are just right.*

continued   Zucchini Zircles with Secret Apricot Sauce

SECRET APRICOT SAUCE

Everything was a secret back in those years. But now, it's out! This sauce is so delicious, you can use it on chicken wings, curried lamb, and deep fried vegetables.

I do believe, actually, that the popularity of the Zucchini Zircles was based entirely on this sauce.

☙ IN A BLENDER, PURÉE:

$^1/_2$ CUP PINEAPPLE JUICE

$2^1/_2$ TABLESPOONS DRY MUSTARD

$1^1/_2$ TABLESPOONS SOY SAUCE

☙ TRANSFER TO A BOWL AND STIR IN:

$1^1/_2$ CUPS APRICOT PRESERVES

DONE.

"That Girl"
Marlo Thomas

"MARILYN, ARE YOU SURE YOU CAN COOK?" HE ASKED

"That Girl"

One day, we got a call from Danny Arnold, the producer of *That Girl* starring Marlo Thomas. He told me Marlo had seen and heard about my clothes at Saks in Beverly Hills and was anxious to meet with me. It was a wonderful meeting. She had a great lean figure with high Mediterranean hips and long legs. Everything she tried on looked great on her, and she truly loved the clothes. Her character was supposed to look lovely, young, and fresh—but without a price tag. These clothes were "perfect for her character Ann-Marie," she told me. I got the show with a single credit card and a big fat check for two outfits per show, times thirteen episodes. *As if I weren't busy enough. But it was an offer I couldn't refuse.*

Everything I made for Marlo, the public wanted. No matter what the age difference. Department stores would get calls about the clothes Marlo wore on her show. It was interesting how many older society women watched that show and then clamored to have the same outfit Marlo wore "two Thursdays ago, please!!"

Marlo was inspirational to me because we both had the same kind of intense life. She produced that remarkable show, starred in it, and employed a lot of people. She was involved in every aspect. In each of our respective fields we were darn good at what we did. We were amused at the occasional pejorative slurs, that strong women like us would receive, such as: "Boy, she's *strong!*" or "She must be hell to work for!" If it had been Lee Iaccoca, he'd have been lauded with superlatives like "What a genius!" "Buy the stock!"

"Her collections are small in comparison to other couturiers, about seventy pieces annually, and have achieved 'instant' success across the country with the smart young fashionables who can afford them—they start at slightly under $400 and soar upward like the red bird. "Outstanding is also the word for the fashions of Cardinali, the design label of Marilyn Lewis, California's newest couturier, and one of the freshest, most original talents to appear on this scene in years."

—Margaret Meade

Photo by Martha Moody.

DANNY THOMAS CHOSE ME TO BE ST. JUDE'S WOMAN OF THE YEAR. MARLO THOMAS AND FAMILY WERE SO PHILANTHROPIC, AND I WORKED HARD FOR THEM.

The clothes were very feminine, but with an edge. Some of the press used words like "avant-garde" to describe them, which pleased me a lot. As the work evolved there seemed to be a little wink, a little naughtiness (just a little) mixed in with the statement. If the humor or the flirtation wasn't there, it didn't get into the collection. Something always had to make you smile.

I remember telling Nancy Reagan she must have been born to the purple because she could stand for hours without fidgeting during a fitting. During those fittings I could see ¹/16 of an inch, if it was off, and I won every bet on that issue. Grading to size is a very important part of good design. Yes, you can go by the books but it doesn't always translate as the sizes get bigger or smaller. You just can't scale things up and down so easily.

In cooking, I had to learn the same thing, that even though you double the recipe, you can't always double the salt. I would see that ¹/16 of an inch and it would make all the difference when it came to making a busty lady look less busty or a hippy lady look less hippy. I think my being a woman and designing for women was an asset in that regard. Fortunately, I had a perfect size 6 figure shaped like a stick. More like a can of Coke I used to say, rather than the bottle. This alone was a plus because the fabric would not get caught up on sensual round protuberances. Breast enhancement was not an issue during those years. It was pretty savvy to look Charlie and Twiggy. Runway models were not shaped with the S-curve at their backside then. They were lean, tall, and flat-chested.

I remember a very wealthy older lady socialite from Palm Beach showing off her new additions, saying that it was her fantasy to "wear no bra and sheer blouses." This was back in the '70s. Not like now, with everyone so obsessed with exercise and body add-ons. All the pattern sizing is off because of this. Even the department stores now have wooden mannequins on display with uplifted glutes and S-curved backsides.

Illustration by Robert Richards.

Illustrations by Robert Richards.

"MARILYN, ARE YOU SURE YOU CAN COOK?" HE ASKED

Times have changed. My sleeve cuts were narrow and high, waistlines tended to be slightly high, which made the body look small. There were many asymmetrical seams and pleats that were snipped so that when a leg was crossed, something wonderful happened. Tweed and satins were mixed. All trademarks of my work.

Eventually, we got Bergdorf Goodman (thanks to Harry) and even made "The Windows on Fifth Avenue." That was awesome. These stores do things beautifully for their patrons and their designers, and show them off in the nicest way. For me, they planned a very high-society charity event with the best New York names including the designer Bill Blass, who was in the audience. After the show, he came over to say, "You know what I like most about your work— there are no gimmicks. The clothes are very pure." I was absolutely thrilled. *It was as if the God of Cloth had spoken.*

I shuttled back to Washington, D.C., and went to work at the bright new Hamlet in Chevy Chase. For an hour I was still in my own reverie about Bill Blass being at my showing and what he had said. Reality set in when I learned that a group of cooks had decided they wanted little "payoffs" from the waitresses. A pack of cigarettes to put out a medium-sized order, and heaven knows what for a large order! They gave those girls

Illustrations by Robert Richards.

such a hard time. I had to stand right up to them and tell them to go. All of them! Who cooked? I did. And the managers. It was my first time on such a long cooking line. Thirty feet long. But we did our best to get that food out, until I was forced to call back to California for help. Harry sent Vern (the director of operations), Joe Lorden (our personnel director), and Jim Tait (a wonderful broiler man). *It was unbelievably naive of me to think that I could have pulled it off alone. They saved me so I could continue my reverie about the God of Cloth.*

At the eighteenth Hamburger Hamlet in Washington, D.C.

"Young, starry-eyed girl hits Hollywood. Takes it by storm with her great designing talent for on-screen costumes. The 'kind' of Marlene Dietrich and Ginger Rogers clothes she always wanted to design from the age of five when all the blank pages in grandmother's books were filled with sketches. Marilyn Lewis, whose Cardinali label has been stitched inside suits and gowns for the past seven years, rewrote the scenario when she met her future husband twenty years ago.

"Sidetracked by marriage and two sons, Adam 16, and David, 19—she helped her husband Harry open seventeen Hamburger Hamlets throughout southern California. Together they have just opened an eighteenth here in Washington but the script has turned full circle and the starry-eyed sketch maker is finally designing clothes.

"Make no mistake about it, Marilyn Lewis supervises every detail of the Hamlets, but she keeps her designer's eye equally on Cardinali enterprises and on a new boutique in Beverly Hills. It was Marilyn Lewis, the designer, who greeted buyers in New York last week to show her new spring-summer line.

'We wanted people in Washington, whose international backgrounds are so diverse, to see an American menu at its best. If we strike a pose of confidence, we do so after 21 years of success,' said Marilyn."

This is JOHN BARRYMORE.
We think he was a great Hamlet!

The HAMBURGER HAMLET

Beverly Hills, Palm Springs, Calif. - Scottsdale, Arizona
Washington, D.C. - Bethesda, Maryland

BARRYMORE AND OUR HAMLETS INTERTWINED.

John Barrymore, Jr. (father of Drew and son of the most famous Barrymore of all, John Barrymore) was so enthralled with our take on the Bard's Hamlet, that one night shortly after we opened he gifted us with a rare treasure: an original sepia-toned photograph of his famous father that had belonged to his grandmother, John Sr.'s mother. It was inscribed "To Mother from her bastard son, John" (1938). In later years when we opened the Chevy Chase Hamlet we placed a beautiful copy on the Barrymore wall.

WITH PHIL GRACE
AT THE AMERICAN
UNIVERSITY, WHERE
WE WERE BOTH
PROFESSORS.

The tristate city of D.C. were so wild about us, they welcomed us every way they could. California Congressman Thomas Rees read us into the Congressional Record and Mr. Phil Grace, who was with the Department of Health Education and Welfare, wrote a welcoming letter, partly because he was also my number one Cardinali fan. He later told me he combed every store all over the country to collect Cardinalis for his wife, which he gave her for her birthday, anniversary, and Valentine's Day. I later learned she didn't appreciate this too much, because she felt controlled by his instinct to want to dress her, though she loved the clothes.

One day the White House called. Pat Nixon wanted to see my collection. Tenner took the call. We had to wait for clearance, not just for me, but for the whole entourage: the models, Tenner, and the hairdresser. Once that came through, we assembled everyone, bought the tickets from Los Angeles to D.C., and flew with all the fiberglass trunks containing the collection. We holed up at the Madison Hotel and waited. Days passed and we were still waiting. The call finally came from the White House to tell us the Nixons had gone to China. Sorry. It was a big tab and a huge letdown. Harry was furious. I don't blame him. Little did we realize that this was the famous getaway to China when all hell had broken loose over Watergate.

Richard Nixon, our president, was in trouble. The Watergate hearings were part of everyone's lunch hour, every day. All the good restaurants installed TV sets for their lunch crowd. It was like Monday night basketball every day. Practically everyone who patronized us at the Chevy Chase Hamlet had a good "inside" story and was indirectly or directly linked to some of the main players. Part of history.

At dinnertime, Judge Sirica would be dining back in the wood-paneled library while Haldeman would be up front sitting at the counter. One night, I was called over by Haldeman. "You don't have your Egg Custard Lulu tonight. You're out of it," he said, complaining. When I told him I was so sorry, but the purveyor had forgotten to deliver the "Lulu" part, which were the graham cracker crumbs, he was much annoyed. He actually shook his finger back and forth at me. "Alibis, alibis!" he muttered. *The Watergate hearings were full of his alibis, alibis. He went to prison.*

EGG   CUSTARD   "LULU"   **SERVES   12**

This was the *custard before crème Brûlée. Check out my John Haldeman "Alibi" story above. Every time I indulge in this lovely, comforting dessert, I think of Haldeman. He evidently thought of it as comforting as well, during Watergate.*

♛ HAVE READY TWELVE 5-OUNCE RAMEKINS OR CUSTARD CUPS.

♛ ALSO HAVE READY A BAIN-MARIE (ROASTING PAN WITH HIGH
   SIDES) THAT WILL FIT THE RAMEKINS OR CUPS.

♛ PREHEAT THE OVEN TO 350°.

♛ IN A MIXING BOWL, WHISK TOGETHER UNTIL EVENLY BLENDED:

continued   Egg Custard "Lulu"

5 LARGE EGGS

1 CUP MILK

1 $^1/_4$ TEASPOONS VANILLA EXTRACT

$^1/_2$ CUP SUGAR

❧ ADD, AND WHISK AGAIN:

1 QUART MILK

❧ POUR THE MIXTURE THROUGH A STRAINER INTO A LARGE
GLASS MEASURING CUP. DIVIDE THE MIXTURE EVENLY INTO
THE CUSTARD CUPS AND SET CUPS INTO THE BAIN-MARIE. ADD
VERY HOT WATER TO COME HALFWAY UP THE SIDES OF THE
CUSTARD CUPS.

❧ BAKE FOR 35 MINUTES IF YOU PLAN TO ADD THE "LULU"
TOPPING (FOLLOWING). BAKE FOR 45 MINUTES IF YOU DO
NOT. THE CUSTARDS SHOULD BE JUST FIRM.

THE "LULU" TOPPING

❧ IN A TOWEL, ROLL AND CRUSH UNTIL FINELY CRUMBLED
(OR WHIZ IN A FOOD PROCESSOR):

16 GRAHAM CRACKERS

❧ PLACE IN A BOWL. ADD AND MIX TOGETHER WELL:

6 TABLESPOONS SWEET BUTTER, MELTED

2 TABLESPOONS SUGAR

❧ SPRINKLE THE "LULU" OVER THE COOKED CUSTARDS AFTER 35
MINUTES IN THE OVEN, AND BAKE FOR 5 MINUTES MORE.
REMOVE THE CUSTARD CUPS CAREFULLY FROM THE PAN AND
COOL TO ROOM TEMPERATURE. REFRIGERATE FOR 2 TO 3
HOURS BEFORE SERVING.

Disappointments

There were too many disappointments. Too many highs and too many lows. Even with all the accolades, I seemed to have nothing left. The press was wonderful to me. My beautiful client list was growing, but I still had nothing left…and I was certainly losing Harry trying to live on both coasts. I made a decision, yet it was to be some time before I could follow it through. I was too young to die. Smoking four packs of cigarettes a day, and plagued with a tight stomach….

There were New York investors who were interested in financing me, but the hitch was I had to move to New York. I couldn't do that. I had a family, a husband, and the strain of being away from each other was beginning to manifest in all kinds of debilitating ways.

It had been ten glorious and nerveracking years in the design business and it was time to return to my roots and my recipes and grow the business that was flourishing now on both coasts. I was tired and saddened. Still, the adjustment was hard, and it would take time.

The Bethesda Hamlet

Landlords came from all over the country trying to attract us. We visited a site in Bethesda, Maryland, that peaked Harry's interest and he wanted to see if my nose would wiggle (which was our marketing tool). It wiggled all right, and we signed the lease. Location? The corner of Democracy and Old Georgetown Road. An onion farm.

The owner wanted to develop a small corner center with the Hamlet as the anchor tenant. It was a fabulous choice. Harry flew back to Los Angeles and I donned my denims and went to work, to build from scratch this time. It was a good distraction; I didn't have to think about Cardinali for a while. Since it was build-to-suit, I developed an all-new Hamlet, suitable for the senators and congressmen who would be our clients. Dark green leather booths instead of the usual red. Instead of terrazzo and carpet, bare shiny wood floors. Beautiful old tapestries from Sotheby's. Winged leather chairs in a warm, nutty brown. Even the tables were oil-stained wood instead of formica. Yes, it was different, and some within our company were shocked. But I couldn't create in a "cookie-cutter" mentality. I wasn't going to allow the "C" word to be used around me. *Chain*. We weren't a chain, we were handmade. The only common thread was that they were all beautiful and comfortable, and shared similar menus.

Bethesda was a bedroom community for some of the most influential people in the Capitol. Our restaurant indeed became their favorite place, and it became the highest-grossing restaurant in our "chain."

JOHN RISKAS' GREEK NOODLES   **SERVES 4**

During our expansion, John was the contractor for many of our Hamlets. These noodles are not Greek. He is.

This is a dish of wide egg noodles that he always laid out on a large platter. Not a bowl. Then he would sprinkle them wildly with Parmesan cheese and black pepper. Then he'd melt unsalted butter with more grated cheese, stir it up and place it under the broiler for a few seconds until the cheese turned into crusty crumbs. As soon as this happened, he would pour this nutty crusty melted butter over all the noodles and serve! We always begged him to make it.

❧ HEAT A PLATTER IN THE OVEN.

❧ 2 (7-OUNCE) PACKAGES MANISHEVITZ WIDE EGG NOODLES

I don't know why, but the Italian wide noodles do not taste as good for this dish.

continued John Riskas' Greek Noodles

⚜ BOIL THE NOODLES ACCORDING TO PACKAGE DIRECTIONS, ADDING 2 TEASPOONS KOSHER SALT TO THE COOKING WATER.

⚜ WHILE THIS IS COOKING, MELT IN A SMALL, OVENPROOF SAUCEPAN:

1 STICK OF SWEET BUTTER

⚜ AND MIX IN:

3/4 CUP PARMESAN CHEESE (IN THE SHAKER)

⚜ PLACE IN A HOT OVEN OR UNDER THE BROILER FOR A FEW SECONDS, AU POINT, UNTIL THE CHEESE TURNS INTO NUTTY BROWN LITTLE CRUNCHIES. DO NOT OVERCOOK!

⚜ DRAIN THE COOKED NOODLES AND LAY HALF OF THEM OUT ON THE HEATED PLATTER.

⚜ SPRINKLE WITH MORE GRATED CHEESE AND LOTS OF BLACK PEPPER. REPEAT WITH THE OTHER HALF OF THE NOODLES. DRIZZLE THE HOT NUTTY CRUSTY BUTTER OVER THE NOODLES AND SERVE IMMEDIATELY.

The Chevy Chase Hamlet was running smoothly, considering it was still rather new. There were still a few problems. Harry left me at the Holiday Inn, where I had set up temporary living quarters. He went back to Los Angeles and I stayed on *and on* to oversee the operations. This was a new role for me, alone in a big important city, knowing no one, except maybe the president and his wife, Nancy, but not that well. It wasn't as if I could call up and say, "Hey, let's go have dinner and a movie, Prez…"

I was totally without a support system of supervisors, managers *and mostly, without Harry.* I thought maybe I could try to wing it alone, but after about ninety days of living at the Holiday Inn, I began to feel the discomfort. I couldn't get a cup of tea in the middle of the night, didn't know whom to call if I were just in need. I thought it might be a good idea if I looked for a small house with a few bedrooms in one of the nice suburbs like Bethesda or Chevy Chase. I had been taught "Bottom line, Bottom line," *but owning real estate within a corporation could be a very wise move.*

Owning a home with a few bedrooms would in the end save us some money, and wouldn't it be fun to have a kind of "Camp Hamlet?" *Wrong! Oh, ode to privacy! But that's another story.* I figured that the support staff could fly in from California and help me for short periods of time and we'd have no extra lodging expense for them.

I found an ideal little home with three floors and four bedrooms in Bethesda, Maryland, directly next door to the Lindy Boggs estate. "Lindy" was Congresswoman Lindy Boggs and mother to the famed ABC correspondent, Cokie Roberts. Their home was a beautiful southern colonial. Mine looked like the servants' quarters in size, but it was just fine.

Harry was busy back in L.A. He was busy planning a big move. Expansion was on and money was needed. We were a hot couple, a hot company, and a hot buy!

When the company went public in 1969, the stock—170,000 shares—came out at $15 and went to $40 in thirty-one minutes! Hot.

They made me Chairman of the Board. This was a surprise move by Harry and Hal Leavitt of Dempsey Tegler. Mr. Leavitt thought it very newsworthy as I would be one of the first female CEOs of a public company in America. *They didn't ask me, they just did it.* Harry would be President.

Merv Griffin had also been invited to be on the board and "almost" accepted with an excited telegram:

However, later something came up in his enormous world and he couldn't join us.

The press had a field day with me. They exaggerated my title to hilarious hyperbole: "The Hamburger Hamlet Queen," "The Doyenne of Hamburgers," "Maharani of the Meatgrinder."

SIA 003 0913A EDT 1 3 JUL 75SR
    SIA135(2013)(2-051360E183)PD 07/02/75 2018
ICS IPMRNCZ CSP
  2134617915 TDRN HOLLYWOOD CA 18 07-02 0818P EST
PMS MRS MARILN LEWIS, CHAIRMAM OF THE BOARD, HAMBURGER HAMLET
, DLR AM, DLR
5319 BRADLEY BLVD
BETHESDA MD 20014
I'M THRILLED, HONORED, EXCITED AND WILLING TO ACCEPT YOUR OFFER.
ALSO I'M VERY HUNGRY COUNT ME IN LOVE
   MERV
NNNN

"We Few, We Happy Few, We Band of Brothers"

—Henry V

We had some very dynamic men on the board, like motion picture producer Howard W. Koch (*Manchurian Candidate, The Odd Couple, Ghost,* recipient of the coveted Thalberg Award) and Victor Carter, major stockholder in Republic Pictures. The selection of Howard Koch was brilliant. He is the most decorated statesman in Hollywood and loved by absolutely everyone in the industry. His honors go on and on. Howard and Victor were very serious board members. Keyed into just the right questions, they made honest decisions. Best was, they saw the big picture. They recognized that building and running restaurants was indeed a live show daily, and only they could appreciate all the nuances that went with that responsibility.

The Howard W. Kochs and the Harry Lewis'.

Photo courtesy of Celebrity-Society.

DAILY ★ NEWS
NEW YORK'S PICTURE NEWSPAPER ®

Vol. 52. No. 291   Copr. 1971 New York News Inc.   New York, N.Y. 10017, THURSDAY, MAY 27, 1971 ●   88

Smashing show measures up to the Cardinali rule

Windbreaker suit (right) in diamond head needlepoint wool has bloused jacket. Colors are blend of green, brown, bone and blue, with coordinated challis blouse. Wine red wool crepe is used for dinner dress (far right). Both costumes from the Cardinali collection by Marilyn Lewis.

Illustrations by Marcos

By KAY THOMAS

Marilyn Lewis, who designs under the label Cardinali in Beverly Hills, is in town this week to show her fall collection.

Although she's been in business just six years, Miss Lewis could teach New Yorkers a thing or two about fashion, especially how to put on a show. Hers preceded an informal lap luncheon in a lovely cool green Plaza suite, the dozen or so spectators sitting on comfortable sofas. It took less than an hour-and-a-half for both lunch and show.

This size 6 glamor girl from the Coast has several distinctions. She never took a design or sewing lesson in her life, she can't sketch, yet she turns out some of the most beautiful clothes available in America today.

While she used to design for her own 5'6" figure, and she still drapes on herself, today she says she always has a particular woman in mind, sometimes much taller, when she makes a costume. In incredibly light weight textured tweeds, she does classic suits with flared or box-pleated skirts, long tailored jackets. Blouses in print silk with wide neckties of the suit fabric add interest to these tailleurs.

Or she will cut a classic reefer in black and white tweed, add a skirt of the same material, then repeat the tweed again in the tie of a white silk blouse.

Many of the designer's coats and suits use snaps instead of buttons, a boon to dressing in this hurried age.

The typical Cardinali skirt, from her boutique collection, is side-slit and often has suspenders of the same material. A metal-looped leather belt is worn diagonally across the hips.

Her day length for skirts is two inches below the knee, with coats to the mid-calf.

At-home and dinner clothes with the Cardinali label come in beautiful embossed velvets, wool georgette, coupe de velour.

These fabrics are used for dinner and theater suits with short or long skirts, or in soft dresses with slightly puffed shoulders. Some dresses are cut with inverted shoulders, so that sleeves lie close to the body.

One pants suit in black shows pants well above the ankle, a long mandarin jacket and a green satin blouse with elasticized peplum which can be tucked in or worn out.

Colors in these evening costumes are somber — black, plum, wine, aubergine.

Included in this collection are several water-color chiffons, hand painted. Intended for the South, these dresses are incredibly simple and lovely and could be worn all year round.

Cardinali clothes can be bought in New York at Bergdorf-Goodman, Saks and Elizabeth Arden. Prices are no more than you would expect for such distinction and beauty.

"President Harry" presented me with an eighteen-karat cushion-cut diamond ring to celebrate the moment. It was so beautiful. *The first piece of jewelry he had ever given me since we met, twenty years before.* It was really something, but it got me in trouble, or maybe it saved my life. We'll talk about that later.

Now, our elevation of the hamburger was nationwide. When I showed my Cardinali collection in New York, I could then shuttle into Washington and pay a visit to the fiefdom before flying back to the West Coast. It was an amazing public relations coup both for Cardinali and for broadening our stock market base.

The board of the Hamlets loved having a sophisticated, high-profile designer-entrepreneur, especially a woman, as Chairman. However, when it came time to chair a meeting, I was scared, a bit tongue-tied. I reverted back to old shyness again. They scripted me, of course, on how to speak to the room full of shareholders. I had to realize that these people were not only shareholders but our customers! As soon as I got that into perspective, I got strong again and was able to get the message out. That helped. I watched their enthusiasm when I got fired up over something. They had clearly come to be entertained as well as watch their investment. So when I felt anger, I showed it. When I felt joy, I shared it.

"MARILYN, ARE YOU SURE YOU CAN COOK?" HE ASKED

This promise to the public could not be broken. The promise became serious business to us. Bottom lines were sacrosanct. It was as if we had taken a vow. Our business became completely different now. You've heard "Location, Location, Location." Now it was "Bottom line, Bottom line, Bottom line." Everything had to be accounted for. Every idea had to be discussed over and over, almost to the point of stilting the creative flow. Lots of money in the till there was, but the free spirit and fun were at a halt. The shareholders were watching, with myopic view focused on our every move.

Harry showed his real calling here. We were growing by leaps and bounds, opening five new restaurants in one year. (Marvin encouraged this madly.) Harry liked wearing a hard hat and his creative juices flowed well when he was negotiating and planning out a new store. We weren't growing like "Topsy" any longer.

At one point, the stock was surprisingly low, selling about $2, and the company thought it a wise idea to buy back the stock, as much as we could get. We put a tender offer out at $4. One of the shareholders thought the offer was too low and should have been at least $6. He brought a class action suit against us. There was no way we could handle this, with every bit of cash needed for expansion.

All the high-priced attorneys were assembled at our Linden Drive house one day, kicking this dilemma around, when I brought a new thought to the table. For some reason, I was always embarrassed to open a new avenue of thought in a full salon of professional men. To offset this, I started with "You may think this is silly, but, why don't we offer them certificates redeemable for food at our restaurants, for the difference?" No one laughed. Bry Danner of Latham and Watkins, a typical think-tank tall guy, smiled slowly, nodding his head, "That might just work…. We could give it a try."

He was very amused at the novelty of the suggestion. The judge who heard the case, as it turned out. was a devoted customer of ours, and he ruled in our favor. He said to the dissident shareholders involved, "This is a very good settlement, gentlemen, as the Hamlets are a wonderful group of restaurants, which you will enjoy."

Time magazine gave this story a few lines; apparently it was newsworthy.

Wake up, Marilyn! Your thoughts can be valuable in a room full of men. Hell, I knew that! Why do I put myself through this??

I was Chairman of the Board of a large group of restaurants now, listed within the top-ranked 100 restaurants doing over $40 million, and it was clear where my efforts should be focused. I simply had to sacrifice my personal achievement as Cardinali in order to continue our stalled personal partnership and "grow" the company. It was painful then, and a great sacrifice for me, even though the sacrifice had paid off to such recognition and to such heights.

A career that so many people, today, twenty-five years later, still remember with great admiration and passion. It does thrill me, I have to admit that it does.

We already had one restaurant open in Chevy Chase, and it was very successful. Bethesda was taking shape. I thought we should look around for more opportunities. That would keep me busy and creative, while I hid for a while and pulled myself together. *I knew I had to make some changes. I didn't know what would do it, but I knew, it couldn't be life in the fast lane, as usual. Smoking four packs of cigarettes a day and living in a world of such demand was like spinning plates in the air on the Ed Sullivan show to the strains of Khatchaturian's "Sabre Dance" from the ballet* Gayne. *Can you see it? Can you hear it?*

It's very hard to be a creative creature, because, when you think you're not being creative, you can be eaten up with the need to be.

The world I was about to give up was glamorous and hard. I mean hard like nails. Maybe my stomach would finally calm down and maybe I didn't have to stay so bloody thin anymore. I knew I'd be out of control fast, with hot fudge sundaes, yummy hamburgers, and chocolate chip cookies.

"But Soft...What Light?"

—Romeo and Juliet

I had wanted to be Cardinali since I was a little girl. It was my dream and now I would have to give it up. It was a shame. I phoned Eleanor Lambert, the most important person in the fashion industry, who had created the coveted Coty Awards. She said, "Oh Marilyn, can't you hang on for one more year? You're so good and the Coty Award cannot be that far away!" *What could I say?*

Even though the Saks chain had lauded my talents and was buying from me in a big way, it was essential to be widely recognized. The press was important. Eleanor Lambert hosted the national press to the best and most

JUDY GARLAND AND SID LUFT.

Photo courtesy of Sid Luft.

noteworthy designers. That's how you read about the designers' collections every season. I needed to be seen by the right people, like Eleanor, in order to be read about, and she did do that for me. She made me very well known. *Judy Garland and Sid Luft, her husband and manager, whom I did not know, made the Eleanor Lambert connection happen. Judy Garland. She was my fashion angel.*

It was a perfect New York Sunday for brunch and Harry was with me. The sidewalks were replete with garbage-stuffed bags on every corner, but it was a good day. A New York Sunday kind of day. Out walking, we chose Maxwell Plum.

There in a corner settee, deep in conversation, were Judy Garland and her husband, Sid Luft. Sid recognized Harry from the Hamburger Hamlets and waved us over. I had never formally met Judy. When she learned that I was the designer Cardinali on *That Girl,* she began raving about my clothes. She went on and on about the lavender "Sachet" dress with its matching parasol in the opening scenes. She called me a genius. "You're the genius," I answered timidly. They asked if Eugenia Sheppard from the *New York Times* had seen my collection. I wearily answered, "No."

"Well, we have to do something about that, don't we, Sid?" Judy responded. "Where will you be later? Where can she see the collection?"

We ran back to the hotel and waited for the call. It came. Sid said that Eugenia was bringing Eleanor Lambert, head of the Coty Awards, with her, and they were coming over by 6:00 P.M. The only problem was that my models were out for the day. It was Sunday, after all. How would I ever be able to pull things together so quickly? But I would pull it together, even if I had to wear the clothes myself! Nothing was going to hamper this opportunity. The models must have felt my angst—they got back to the hotel just at the right time.

When it was over, Eleanor called someone and said, "You have to come over and see this collection. You know when the California designers are good, they're good!" (She was referring to Galanos, Gernreich, and Jean Louis.) It was a typical New York kind of backhanded compliment, but it was important. Soon I was invited to show to "The World Press" in New York with all the big boys, Geoffrey Beene, Bill Blass, and Donald Brooks. It was a blast and it opened doors everywhere for me. Now I had a chance for the Coty Award somewhere along the line and the endorsements that a designer lives and breathes on. *But it came too late.*

The more the press wrote how wonderful the Cardinali collection was, the harder it seemed to do the next one. The benchmark kept getting higher and higher. I was meeting the challenges but the toll on my health was looming large. I was too young to be taking Donnatal, Bentyl, Phenobarbital, for all kinds of digestive disturbances. And smoking four packs of cigarettes a day!

The Individual

It is an age of individuality and CARDINALI is in step. Not only is her collection an individual one, but each style within it stands on its own look, does its own thing.

Dependably, it is the right thing. Sketched, a costume which merges the fanciful with the elegant. Printed chiffon is a flutter with pleats from bare strapped bodice to hem. Colorful embroidery gives a high fit to the dress, bands a short jacket.

"The spirit of the Cardinali collection is unique. Perhaps the key is that it's designed by a woman, who understands women's basic desires to be both 'with it' and utterly feminine. A touch of the theatrical for special occasions....The Cardinali collection also includes the most exciting little black cocktail dresses seen in years of color. Whether they're lace or silk, they're figure-defining and enchantingly feminine. If anything is going to bring back black, it's these dresses."

—Eugenia Sheppard, the New York Times

Illustrations by Robert Richards.

Illustrations by Robert Richards.

Public Relations Release from Eleanor Lambert, of the Coty Awards:

"The fact (and we're so proud of it) that Cardinali has become a nationally known name in only four years is not because we've been such fashion-watchers, but because we're such girl-watchers. I have a certain hang-up about designing. Cardinali designer Marilyn Lewis says, 'I don't think about what *fashion* is, but what a *woman* is. Being one myself, I know that first of all we're chameleons. For a woman of imagination to settle for one type of clothes would be like eating nothing but mashed potatoes. She wants caviar and peanut butter, and the moon and stars on toast. She is never less than four women—the demure one, the brisk one, the woman-plus, and the man-killer.'"

CARDINALI

"Cardinali, Edith Head, Mr. Blackwell, George Whittaker, and Bill Theiss." — TV Guide "Five Designers," October 1968. *Do you remember my dream to meet Edith Head? I finally did.*

"It Is a Melancholy of Mine Own"

—As You Like It

I went home. Cardinali had to end. There was too much going on.

But going home didn't work. It was a strange place for me. We had a beautiful home and a thriving business, with a fabulous reputation, but I was getting that "feeling" again. That I was a "business machine." The "clutch" solving endless problems. I was with my wonderful husband, who was a born workaholic. Everywhere I went, someone came up to me to ask about Cardinali, and if I was ever going to design again. It was a pain in my heart when I answered, "No. No more." I was in withdrawal. I knew I had to hide for a while, because I was, frankly, in a depression. A funk. I flew back to Washington. To watch over things.

Ronald Reagan was in the White House. I began to be invited to a few Washington embassy parties, and to the White House, which was interesting for me. Social protocol was strict. One drink more was noticed. Being ten minutes late was noticed. One did not show partisan preferences. Dress was pure Elizabeth Arden, and hair: Blonde was good, but never, never too red. (For God's sake, wash some of that red out of your hair, Marilyn! It's not a Washington color!) I was there to grow our business. I was there to give America a fine-looking place to serve a hamburger to the visiting dignitaries. (Those are the people who could park and double-park anywhere they wanted.)

With Nancy Reagan.

This led to the State Department using the Hamlet to entertain foreign dignitaries in order to show them what an American hamburger was all about. Until
us, there were only greasy spoons to deal with. I met so many congressmen and
senators and judges. One might say I became well connected. Julius Bengston,
Mrs. Reagan's devoted hairdresser who traveled all over the world with her,
began squiring me around town. Julius had also done several Cardinali shows for
me back in L.A. It was he who had invited Nancy to see my collections back
when she was first lady of our state, California.

*Her big black limo with the American flag on it would pull up in front of our
home in Beverly Hills and a strapping state trooper driver would escort Nancy to our
door. Every time she came, our houseman, Lauro, would strangely disappear. It got*

"Don't go anywhere, we need a cup
of tea for Mrs. Reagan...."

very embarrassing. I'd be showing Mrs. Reagan the collection and would try to get her
a cup of tea or some water and Lauro would evaporate into thin air! When I asked him
why he was never around when Mrs. Reagan came to the house, he answered, "When
I saw the state car coming into the driveway with that American flag on it, I thought
it was Immigration!"

Lauro had been hired directly from the Philippines by Ann Hamilton Spalding,
George Hamilton's mother, for their big estate. One day, Anne, who wore my Cardinali

designs, called to ask if we needed a houseman. She was moving to Palm Beach, and he had been a wonderful employee. We met and loved him at first sight. The year was 1969 and we certainly did need him. Lauro is of course a citizen now, and still with us after thirty years.

Immersed in building four new restaurants, watching our stock rise, reporting to the board of directors and learning the Washington, D.C. protocol, handling crisis seating during Watergate, *and* teaching a four-credit course in marketing at American University kept me enormously busy. No one thought about Cardinali too much.

Photo by Anthony Howarth.

When I was invited to teach a four-credit course at American University, this was my opening, to the class of fifty students: (The class was called "Owning Your Own Business, An American Dream.")

"The restaurant business has all the dynamics of show business. The dynamics of law, of marketing, of public relations, accounting, and the dynamics of behavioral science. It is exciting, aggravating, and if you are ready to lurch from one earth-shattering crisis to another, work seven days a week while you never felt younger or happier, then you'll know you've chosen your life's work correctly. The best part about the whole thing for me? I can now afford the dentist."

THE AMERICAN UNIVERSITY INTERNS.

FRANK SINATRA LEADS MRS. RONALD REAGAN INTO THE CENTURY PLAZA. NANCY REAGAN IN RED CARDINALI CHIFFON GOWN.

THE DESIGN FOR NANCY REAGAN'S DRESS.

Harry was on the West Coast. I was on the East Coast. And no husband, again.

From time to time, I was invited to the White House. Saw Nancy Reagan, who wore many of my designs when she was first lady of California. She was always very dear and friendly, as was the president. She remembered me from the early Westwood Hamlet, where she and the president had been courting and, of course, holding hands. They were so beautiful together. Two actors, she in her espadrilles and long, full-circle "broom" skirts.

When the service industry was badly hit with the impact of the Declaration of Tip Tax,

HERE I WAS IN CAP AND GOWN, IN THE RAIN. DURING THE COMMENCEMENT EXERCISES AND PROFESSOR'S PROMENADE. I FELT LIKE LUCILLE BALL PLAYING ME IN A MOVIE.

the White House gave me Michael Deaver to lend an ear to my opposition. The bartenders, waiters, and waitresses were stunned by this new tax. I felt that it was a flawed plan because it was not targeted at any other tipped group, such as hairdressers, taxi drivers, dining room captains, or maitre d's. It was nice that Michael Deaver was listening. He couldn't have been more sympathetic. I found him to be a charming person who liked talking recipes, just as I did. He swapped a cheese soup recipe with me that was delicious, but laden with cholesterol. The meetings with him enabled me to have staff meetings with the waiters and waitresses on both coasts. They were impressed that I was trying to do something, and it helped me illustrate that we were being heard within the system. *I should have said we were being humored by the system. The restaurant lobby went to work against the tax, but were able to do nothing about it.*

Flying back and forth every thirty days from one coast to the other to keep my legal domicile intact, and keep an eye on my husband was an uneasy lifestyle.

This was not what I had had in mind.

I remember whispering to Harry, "Try not to fall in love with anyone." And then I left again. This life was hard for both of us. No one needs a true test like this. Once you're a public company, there's only one word to live by: growth. And grow we did. I set our revenue stream at $50 million and said, "Then, maybe, I could come home."

Harry was stable and a wonderful partner, yet the beautiful business we were creating was tearing us apart. Long-distance relationships do not work! Concentrating our activities to one or two areas within close proximity would have netted the same results: a lot of money. The same money that flying all over hell-and-gone had produced.

A Model Employee

James McWhorter was his name. An eighteen-year-old busboy at the new Bethesda Hamlet. He was so good that we had to move him into cooking. Then he was so good at that, we had to move him into management. He was so good at that, I wanted to adopt him!

Seriously.

A train had killed his parents, and his aunt was raising him. I thought he should go on to college and "become" something, but his aunt would have no part of me adopting him. Jimmy enrolled in my class at American University. He continued to work for us, in all his capacities, for about ten years. One day, when I was back on the West Coast, he called to tell me he was going into the produce business, and wondered if he could have the D.C. area Hamlets' business?

There were then four. "Yes, of course!" I was thrilled to say.

Today he has many trucks and is the quality purveyor to the top restaurants in the Capitol area, grossing several million a year. Never afraid to do any job. And he made it! My American Dream worked for him in a big way.

DANCING WITH JIM McWHORTER AT THE AMERICAN UNIVERSITY GRADUATION PARTY.

Our Nation's Capital

Washington, D.C., was humorous in its way. The press column everyone read was called "The Ear," and the writer had real fun with everyone she wrote about. With me, she coined the phrases "The Doyenne of Hamburgers," "Maharani of the Meatgrinder," and wrote "Look for red hair, good clothes, and lots of big white teeth." The Russians at the embassy parties were so serious as they'd tell you, in all sincerity, that their job in this country was to inform Moscow about every TV show on the air and its content, including cartoons.

White House access was as secure as an airport check. Metal detectors, pat-downs and purse checks, but not if you entered with a wheelchair. Not only did you sail through, without address, but your "wheelchair pusher" as well. I wanted

THE EAR

LEAVE 'EM LAUGHING . . . Catholic U biggies plotting their Inauguration Brunch are outraged, Ear hears. One buzzed the White House last week to ask the time of the Reagan Oath. "Don't know," snapped a White Houser, with a small Oath of his own. "Try the Inaugural Office. And no, we don't know their number." Slam. A little Charity, please, Catholic Uers. White Housers have worries galore. To put it bluntly, darlings, they still haven't figured out just how to whisk Jimmy Carter from the scene after Ronnie's Oath. "A helicopter's Out. A throng stormed Jerry Ford as he got in his, remember," moans one Worried One, "They almost knocked that whirly thing off the top." (Ear's positive he means off the top of the 'copter. These are Serious People we're talking to.) "On the other hand, we can't just have Carter wandering off into the crowd, can we? " Oh, dear. It's bad enough worrying about getting In, let alone Out. *Now* Ear will watch that space and worry.

THE BURGER COURT . . . Hamburger Hamlet queen Marilyn Lewis and hubby Harry will trip to town for the hoopla and the Big Ball. Ear bets you didn"t know that they're Reagan Buddies from Hubby Harry's old days at Warner Brothers. (Harry, actually, was in about 300 movies, some of them with Ronnie, but he was always just part of the posse.) Marilyn herself, meanwhile, before becoming Maharani of the Meatgrinder, was dubbed "Cardinale," and designed frocks galore for Nancy. You can't get much Inner than that, Earwigs, without an awful lot of work.

MORSELS FOR YOUR MEMORY BOOK . . . . Panic at the Smithsonian: The museum can't show Nancy's Inaugural Ball gown among its other First Ladies for simply months. (It takes at least six months to nail together a proper Dummy of the First Lady to sport the Outfit, you know.) To fill the gap, Nancy's giving a sub: Her famed Republican Convention Suit. (Oatmeal-beige Adolpho knit, nattily edged with chestnut braid. Remember how we ooohed?) This, darlings, will be sported by a vaguely Nancyesque dummy — not, of course, loitering all out-of-place among the ball-gowned Mamies and Jackie, but in a tasteful glass case all by itself. It will remain 'til the Almost-Real Nancy Reagan can stand up. Uncle Oscar plans to drop by for a chat every now and again. He's getting worse. Tomorrow: Merely Ear.

THE WASHINGTON STAR Monday, January 12, 1981

to tell someone about this, for fear of harm to the president, but it got complicated. A homeless lady slept in a huge trash bin at the gate of the White House, directly opposite the guard house. The lid of the trash bin would mysteriously rise and lower, as you entered. No one seemed to mind. She may still be there.

Amy Carter left no tips. Neither did the secret service.

I was living in Bethesda next door to Cokie Roberts and the Boggs family. They made good watching. They had their own gas pump in their yard, which I was certain would blow up one day and extinguish us all.

Chicago and Scottsdale, Arizona, were next for my nonstop expansion program. I was determined to build them up, stay awhile, and get home. *Instead, I was kidnapped.*

CHICAGO: "BE WARY THEN; BEST SAFETY LIES IN FEAR"

—Hamlet

It was my own fault. I walked right into it with my eyes wide open and my mouth closed shut. That voice on the phone tricked me and I fell for it. I was out there too much. A woman alone in a big city. Too much exposure. Too much publicity. I believe it's a gender thing. Let's face it, there are certain freedoms men have that women shouldn't even want!

I arrived in Chicago to set up a new base. On the very first night there, who did I meet? The most prominent couple in town: Irv and Essie Kupcinet. They were so famous that the city renamed the Wabash Street Bridge the Irv Kupcinet Bridge. Irv wrote a column for the *Sun Times* called "Kup's Corner." Every movie star, sports star, and political celebrity made it their business to know the Kupcinets. They had endured their own personal tragedy, when their young daughter was murdered in Hollywood while pursuing a film career.

It was assumed Karen was killed by an actor with whom she had recently broken up. A crime never solved.

The Kupcinets made their way over to say hello to me as they were leaving the restaurant Crickets and welcomed me to the city. They had seen the big *Fortune* magazine article (which displayed me in a bikini holding a business meeting around the pool) and recognized me. "How did you recognize me with my clothes on?" I asked, laughing. We liked each other from the beginning and when they threw a party or were going out to dinner with someone special, like Frank Sinatra, I was often included.

They became my family away from home. That's one thing about the people of Chicago. They love new people and include you in everything. We embarked on a plan to photograph society figures in our monthly ad in the *Chicago* magazine. In the end, we didn't have to call them. They called us. Philanthropists, artists, ballet people, business people, and beautiful people. They wanted to be included!

When the Chicago Hamlet opened, we gave the big annual birthday party for Bonnie Swearingen, wife of John Swearingen, who was Chairman of the Board of Standard Oil. It was black tie at the Hamlet for the crème de la crème of high finance. It was very amusing for them, and the public relations factor was phenomenal. A good hamburger: the social equalizer among the hoi polloi.

HARRY AND I WITH THE KUPCINETS.

Photo courtesy of Celebrity-Society.

The Helene Curtis Company was headquartered in Chicago, and they invited me to sit on their board. The scion of the family, Ron Gidwitz, was drop- dead movie-star gorgeous and married to top model Christine Kemper (a face on every cover). To be on their board was an extraordinary opportunity for me. On my own board I had to report, respond, and sometimes apologize if we didn't meet expectations. *Stomach-ache time.* On this board, I could sit back like a student and listen, learn. Dealing with glamour, marketing, labor, strikes, ecology and by-products, waste and usage—it was a real learning curve.

I found that my métier was in asking good marketing questions. Once, I offered a very synergistic *I thought* plan to expand into the pet shampoo business (for those who want to share the very best with their pets). The Board thought it could have an adverse effect. And who knows, they may have been right. Having the Gidwitz family and the Kupcinet family in my life seemed very good, and it was. Chicago was a home. Another city, not my own.

"Chicago Is a Razor's Edge— Watch Your Step, Lady!"

—A Chicago Cabbie

The Chicago press wanted to photograph me for every holiday issue: Valentine's Day, Christmas. If the holiday was red, it became my day. *There are some benefits to being a redhead.* They photographed me in my kitchen, cooking; they were interested in my charities; the way I entertained, my philosophies—and of course the big question: Where did I shop? (Ultimo, of course). All because I was a successful businesswoman. *Like I was the first?!?* I posed willingly and easily, foolishly, wearing my beautiful big eighteen-karat diamond ring. I was stupid. Certainly not thinking. It had been ten years that I wore that ring. Wore it with everything. *I deserved it, I thought, because I was so wonderful.* It was a part of me. To most, it probably did not look real, but all it takes is one person to figure out that it was. *I was about to be kidnapped!*

Thinking back, I can sense where it may have started. It was on the *Good Morning Chicago* show, which Steve Edwards hosted (just before Oprah Winfrey joined him). Someone saw that ring and made a plan.

The phone rang. It was a Mr. Johnson. He said he was a producer at CBS. He had "seen me on TV" and "was very impressed," enough to want to screen-test me for my own show. I was, of course, flattered, but told him that I had no interest in having my own show, as I was busy enough opening restaurants all over the country, that I was already on overload. But he wouldn't take no for an answer and suggested that I think about it. He'd "call back in a couple of days."

He asked that I keep this quiet since, if I did decide to do this, I would be unseating Lee Phillips Bell (who, with her husband, Bill Bell, had created and produced the shows *The Young and the Restless* and *The Bold and the Beautiful*). Lee Phillips had her own talk show, and I would probably be replacing her, he

said, "if I possessed conversational ability." I took it with a grain of salt and was not very interested. But Mr. Johnson persisted, calling me at least twice a week over a period of three months. I remember telling him that I had to fly to Arizona to watch over the construction of our newest restaurant, and I then had to fly to Atlanta to spend some time there, watching over the Hamlet that had just opened. He responded with "I guess we're just going to have to hogtie you, aren't we?" I thought he had a strange sense of humor. *I didn't realize how literal he was.*

Finally, after three months of turning him down, I relented. I left him a message *at CBS*. He sent the limo. It was February and the snow was deep. The limo crawled through the streets to get to CBS. But it passed CBS.

"Where are we going?" I asked.

"We're going to pick up Mr. Johnson," the driver answered.

I knew something wasn't right, but I was motionless, totally unable to move. It was like an out-of-body experience. *Watching yourself, physically unable to do anything about what seemed to be happening. Like screaming, but no sound is coming out.*

We pulled slowly into the back of the Twin Marina Towers. The door locks sprung up all at once. *I can still hear them.*

Three masked gunmen entered the car with lightning speed, handcuffed me to the backseat of the car and demanded my ring, with "mother fuckers" flying at the beginning and the end of every command. As in "You scream, you die, mother fucker!!" The gunmen were skinny, extremely nervous, and white. Their ski masks were black. The driver waddled off to a waiting van, as if he were padded. *He looked like Martin Balsam, the actor (in* Psycho*), running. That's all I remember.* Several hours later, some black-and-white squad cars arrived on that deserted patch of parking lot and set me free. I was still numb. In shock. They took me to the police station to be debriefed and to look at mug shots. I recognized no one. The next day, the paparazzi were encamped in my lobby and would not leave. I was on the front page of every newspaper for two weeks, and FBI agents were my constant visitors.

Several weeks later, the Kupcinets took me to the Pump Room at the Ambassador East Hotel to have dinner with their very good friend Sidney Korshak, a labor lawyer who had many Las Vegas clients. I was to tell my story to him during dinner, and he would then make a phone call to Las Vegas to see if they might know where my diamond had ended up, or if permission to do the job came through their domain. Vegas gave him a clean bill of health. *God had spoken. It was so odd.*

Mayor Bilandic and his wife, Heather, wrote me a nice note. They were sorry such a thing had happened to me in their town. The Chicago police offered escorts, free of charge, to accompany me to any social event I cared to attend. *Little did I know the FBI was playing games with me.* I too played detective, by insisting the FBI get all the call-out telephone sheets from CBS, so we could scan them to see if there were calls made to me or to my restaurant. They looked at me as if to say, "You can't ask CBS for that! This is an enormous entity, a sacred cow."

Mr. Johnson, it turned out, was a janitor at CBS, which is why when I called for him to cancel one of the appointments we had made, I got a call back. But not from the janitor, Mr. Johnson. Poor dear man, he had nothing to do with it. How that telephone relay worked is still baffling. How clever of the perpetrator to use the name of a janitor who was well known to the CBS switchboard. They, of course, would take a message for Mr. Johnson. But how did the phony Mr. Johnson get that message to call me? We figured it was the driver who was the mastermind, or the Mr. Johnson, since he was without blindfold. He was not in any mug shot, which meant he had no record and that, therefore, allowed him to show his face. *Most of all, I remember the back of his ears. They were cauliflower-like.*

Bill Kurtis, CBS news commentator at the time, was reporting the story one night on the 6:00 news, and he added a little aside: "CBS wouldn't do this to such a nice lady." I was in such shock during the days that followed, that when one of the FBI men, asked me where I was born, I could not answer him. I did not know where I was born. I could not remember Cleveland. It was temporary, called global amnesia. I finally got my mind back about three weeks later. The FBI learned that the limo had been stolen about three months earlier from a supermarket parking lot, and had been hidden in the town of Cicero. *That alone is chilling. Three months.*

One day, The FBI men asked me to put on dark glasses, a wig, and a babushka. They wanted to take me somewhere to identify someone walking across the street. To see if I could "recognize the walk." We drove in a beat-up van, like something out of *Serpico*. It had torn curtains and peepholes. What struck me as strange was that the driver of this junk-heap van, an FBI agent, was in full view, wearing a spiffy blue blazer, shirt, and rep tie. "Stay down! Stay down!" he would yell, and I would drop.

We drove into a schoolyard and picked up a slender man with fine Italian features, wearing a white linen suit. He looked like the Italian actor Vittorio Gassman, and identified himself as a customs officer. We made eye contact, which made me feel clammy down the back of my neck. But I was in disguise. When we got to Cicero, we parked across from a Lincoln dealership. I was given a pair of binoculars and asked to look through one of the holes in the curtains, to watch the customs officer walk across the street. *One of my eyes is nearsighted and the other farsighted, which made binocular viewing very difficult, particularly through a tiny hole in the curtain and on your belly.* "Does his walk look familiar to you?" they asked. I answered negative. "Does he look familiar to you?"

"I'm not sure...there is something...but, I'm not sure." I was afraid to say much more. We waited an hour, while the customs officer paced back and forth, as if waiting for someone. He came back to the van and announced that "they weren't showing up." (Whoever "they" were.) We drove him back to the school-yard. He got out, handed me his business card, and told me to call him if anything came up. I was driven home. I still cannot tell you what went down that day, except to say, that I did try the number on the card to find there was no such number and I never saw the customs officer again. Not even at the airport.

I was obsessed. I couldn't think of anything else. My mind was playing tricks on me: at airports and other public places, I would see the driver, wherever I was. In my dreams, I kicked his ass! Why didn't I open the door and jump out while he was plodding through all that snow? Why didn't I notice that the limo's engine was hot-wired? Why did I obey such a scam, and not breathe it to a soul, just to protect a talk show hostess?

Two years later, I was watching 20-20. They were doing a piece on a Chicago mole. It was the driver! I'm almost certain. They said he may have murdered a woman in Florida, and that he was also involved in jewel heists, but no one would prosecute him, because he was a mole for the FBI! I called Kup immediately. He advised me to forget it, unless I wanted to end up in the back of some car, beheaded!

"Love All, Trust a Few"

—All's Well That Ends Well

It's great for the ego to read about yourself all the time, especially when you run a public company and so much press is yours for the asking. Free advertising for the company, yes, but it is probably better advice to be very selective and a bit quieter. I waited many years to have such an earned award on my finger. Now I wear almost nothing. *Now and then, I think that the adornment may have saved my life and I get tempted. That's women for you. Chameleons.* Whenever I wax poetic about how I love Chicago, I remember that cabbie telling me, "Chicago is a razor's edge—watch your step, lady."

Who had planned this against me? Who had set me up? Was it my secretary? My hairdresser? The men in the lobby? The valets? The manager at our restaurant? Another restaurant? The jeweler, where I once left my diamond to be cleaned? Someone I thought I could trust? It was a bad habit of mine to take so many people in, to let them see too much. I had a tendency to be very open with the people around me, but it backfired when they realized how fragile I was. Then, the usual reaction was to mother me, and get on my little girl's side. *To feel like a little girl was the best feeling in the world. A place where I didn't have to make any decisions, or think so hard. It was here I could laugh and giggle. Inside the little girl, I could get near to crying. Being so strong for so many years, blocking out the hurts as if they weren't happening, had taken its toll. I had found my hiding place, in the kitchen.*

Harry was in California. He could not be there for me. I was afraid if he came to Chicago, it would happen again. Neither of us were making any sense. He was shaken as well. I had lost the ability to take charge of my life. Temporarily.

My shortfall of strength and conviction was creating an eddy, a vortex of unexpected curves and turns. Arizona had been built during this problematic stage and it didn't catch the wave of success anticipated. I felt doomed. Every decision I made seemed wrong and inaccurate. Jimmy Carter was in office, interest rates were soaring, and gasoline prices were in the stratosphere, so everyone stopped driving! This affected Arizona's tourist business. Our new business suffered. It was my first failure.

To borrow a line from Rich Little: "How can I open a small business in this city?" Answer: "Open up a large one and wait." Arizona, like Texas, gave me the feeling of great expanse, of spreading out. Build it bigger and bigger, wider and wider. I pure-and-simply overdesigned it, until I got lost in it and it got lost in me. Had I stuck with our successful formula, stayed with the protocol, and acted more conservatively, we might have withstood the gas hike and the over-the-top interest rates.

Arizona had to close. The first time for all of us, who had been on an unstoppable roller coaster of success.

Closing a restaurant is painful. Closing any business is painful. It's something we must learn to do without looking back, however. As Chairman of the Board, I had to be the strong one. Learn from the experience. Take the blame and move on. I discussed this with my students at the American University during my tenure there. Is it emotional? Of course it's emotional. "I can think of thousands of things I did wrong, considering the state of mind I was in. You must try to keep this in perspective and not repeat the errors," I told them. "That's all you can do. Make new mistakes. But try to stick with the proven program, especially when feeling indecisive or unsure."

You can always loosen or tighten the screws when you get your legs back.

Photo by Jack O'Grady.

BLACK TIE BRISKET
AND COFFEE BASTING SAUCE

SERVES 8

In the 1950s I taught myself to cook the brown foods of the '50s.

I started by learning what you can do with a good beef stock (like pot-au-feu, onion soup, brisket broth with vegetables…endless).

Once you have beef stock down, you can talk turkey with any chef. Here, we make a brisket broth, and serve the brisket alone or with a soup made from the leftover broth.

BLACK TIE BRISKET

Benjamin, our eight-year-old grandson (and a vegetarian) told me, "I'm going for seconds on the brisket, Cookie Mama, it's the best steak I ever ate!"

We like to serve this, our "take" on pot-au-feu, with glazed duck sausages, veal sausage nuggets, roasted chicken thighs, sauerkraut, green pickle relish (salsa verde), and mashed potatoes—wow, what a feast!

5- TO 6-POUND FIRST-CUT BEEF BRISKET

WATER AS NEEDED

2 LARGE ONIONS, PEELED, SCORED AT THE TOP, AND IMPALED
    WITH 6 CLOVES GARLIC

2 TEASPOONS SALT

12 BLACK PEPPERCORNS

2 TEASPOONS CELERY SALT

1 CARROT, 1 STALK CELERY, A LITTLE BUNCH OF PARSLEY

WONDERFUL, PUNGENT COFFEE BASTING SAUCE (RECIPE FOLLOWS)

BRISKET BROTH

continued   Black Tie Brisket and Coffee Basting Sauce

☙ Place brisket in a 6 ½ quart heavy roaster or Dutch oven (I like Le Creuset) and cover with water, 8 or 9 cups. Add onions, salt, peppercorns, and celery salt. Bring to a full boil and immediately lower the heat to a simmer. Skim off the impurities. Add the vegetables and cover tightly. Simmer *only* for 3 hours.*

☙ (If using an oval roaster, cook gently over two burners). Remove the meat to a carving board to rest and cool down. Refrigerate the meat until thoroughly chilled. Strain the broth and place, uncovered in the freezer for 1 hour, to solidify the fat. You should have about 9 cups of rich beef broth. Slice the meat only when it is chilled.

*Remember, to simmer means to keep the water moving. It must not be still. But it must not be madly bubbling.

☙ Slicing the brisket is part of the art: start on the point of the brisket. What you want is a "diamond pattern" to the cut—slant your knife so it looks like it's starting with a thicker slice, but slants inward to make a thinner cut. You'll see how it feels and you'll understand it more than I can try to write it.

☙ The important thing is to turn the meat the minute you see the grain changing to straight line strings. Turn it to another angle to get back to the "diamond" pattern slice. Carefully trim all the fat off each slice. Lay into a baking dish on a slant overlapping the slices. Guests will normally take two to three slices.

☙ Now paint the top of the brisket slices with the Pungent Coffee Basting Sauce, page 180. Carefully add

A CUP OF THE STRAINED BEEF BROTH AROUND THE EDGES.
COVER WITH PLASTIC WRAP AND REFRIGERATE OVERNIGHT.
REMOVE AT LEAST 2 HOURS BEFORE YOU WANT TO SERVE.

♛ PREHEAT THE OVEN TO 325°. REMOVE THE PLASTIC WRAP AND
REPLACE WITH FOIL. REHEAT IN THE WARM OVEN FOR JUST
ABOUT AN HOUR. UNTIL NICE AND HOT.

PUNGENT COFFEE BASTING SAUCE

I TABLESPOON FINELY GRATED ONION, JUICE AND ALL

I TEASPOON FINELY MINCED GARLIC

I TEASPOON COARSELY GROUND BLACK PEPPER

I TEASPOON INSTANT COFFEE POWDER

2 TABLESPOONS BROWN SUGAR

2 TABLESPOONS WORCESTERSHIRE SAUCE

$^1/_2$ CUP CATSUP

♛ MIX ALL TOGETHER WELL. YIELD: 3/4 CUP, JUST ENOUGH FOR
ONE FIRST-CUT BLACK TIE BRISKET.

FINISHING THE BRISKET BROTH

*You have only used 1 cup of the wonderful brisket broth to reheat the
brisket. Here is what you do with the rest. This serves 12 people.*

REMAINING BROTH FROM THE COOKED BRISKET

6 MEDIUM CARROTS, CUT DIAGONALLY IN LARGE CHUNKS

6 STALKS CELERY, CUT DIAGONALLY IN LARGE SLICES

2 TO 3 TABLESPOONS CHOPPED PARSLEY

I LEEK, WHITE PART ONLY, SLICED

continued Black Tie Brisket and Coffee Basting Sauce

3 BEEF BOUILLON CUBES

4 CUPS WATER

༄ AFTER FREEZING THE STRAINED BROTH TO SOLIDIFY THE FAT, AND REMOVING ALL OF IT, LET THE BROTH STAND OVERNIGHT IN THE REFRIGERATOR. SKIM OFF ANY ADDITIONAL FAT AND DISCARD. PLACE THE BROTH IN A LARGE KETTLE AND ADD THE CARROTS AND CELERY, INCLUDING THEIR LEAVES, THE PARSLEY, AND LEEK. DISSOLVE THE BOUILLON CUBES IN WATER AND ADD TO POT. COVER AND SIMMER OVER LOW HEAT FOR 1 HOUR. SERVE AS A SOUP WITH ALL THE VEGETABLES. THE STRAINED BROTH MAY BE USED AS THE BASIS FOR OTHER SOUPS, SUCH AS CLASSIC POT-AU-FEU OR ONION SOUP (PAGE 87).

ITALIAN GREEN PICKLE SAUCE (SALSA VERDE)

This is wonderful over boiled beef brisket, chicken, or fried fish.

12-OUNCE JAR SWEET GREEN PICKLE RELISH

1/2 CUP BASIC VINAIGRETTE*

༄ WHISK TOGETHER UNTIL SMOOTH.

*BASIC VINAIGRETTE

3 TABLESPOONS RED WINE VINEGAR

6 TABLESPOONS GOOD EXTRA VIRGIN OLIVE OIL

DASH EACH OF SALT AND BLACK PEPPER

"You Can Go Home Again"

Photo by Wallace Seawell.

PART THREE

"The Web of Our Life Is of a Mingled Yarn, Good and Ill Together"

—All's Well That Ends Well

This time, it really was time to come home. I wanted my life back. The life we had before, when we were a couple. It seemed to me that Harry felt less threatened when I worked at his side. *It wouldn't be easy, especially since Harry is a handsome man and a lot of women were hoping I'd stay away forever.* To be married and in business together is very hard. To work all day with your husband, then go home to romance. This is hard to process. We were both in disconnect mode. A different kind of love emerges. A strong love, like between best friends. And that's what you are, of course, but tedium takes its course. I was told by many that it was the character of marriage to lose the passion, but gain strength in the union. Looking back, I would have traded it all to have had more growth with Harry. As strange as it may sound, Harry seemed to be running faster than I was.

It was Harry who wanted to keep opening new places. It was me who was trying to slow him down. I wanted each place we opened to flourish through nurturing and careful watching. It wasn't my style to create and run. I liked setting goals, but the level of perfection was getting higher and higher. Running our business like two Olympiad athletes going for the gold. I must admit it was gratifying, but hard on the id. We had both propelled our lives into such a fervor that there was nothing left over but the endless treadmill, moving at ever greater speeds. I knew I couldn't just stop, it was not my nature; but I wanted to try to reshape our lives. Our business life had moved ahead of our personal relationship. *It never occurred to us to be careful what we wished for.*

We were a little tentative about our new union, the starting over. It was just the two of us now. The boys had left the nest, and the house seemed so much bigger. David was in Vienna and Adam in Minneapolis, a married man raising

"Designer Marilyn Lewis (Cardinali) was one of thirteen women selected for 1968 'Woman of the Year' honors bestowed this week by the *Los Angeles Times*. Mrs. Lewis, who is Chairman of the Board of Hamburger Hamlets Inc., in addition to operating her own couture business and running a home for her husband and two sons, was described as a 'bottomless well of energy' by *Times* Society Editor Maggie Savoy. Others receiving the distinction this year were Mrs. Ronald Reagan, actress Greer Garson, Judge Shirley M. Hufstedler, TV producer Carolyn Raskin, Democratic national committee woman Carmen Warschaw, Republican national committeewoman Dorothy Wright Nelson, professor Marija Gimbutas, writer Joan Didion, swimming champion Debbie Meyer, and cultural and charity workers Mrs. John Connell and Mrs. George Vernon Russell."

—Los Angeles Times

Photo by Pat Munn, *Palm Springs Life.*

THIS PHOTO APPEARED WITH A PROFILE OF ME BY PAT MUNN, IN *Palm Springs Life*.

a family. Picking up the personal pieces strewn in the wake of my path to success was going to be no easy task. The year was 1984. I had been away for a long time. Yet nothing had changed. *I had married an actor who happened to be a remarkable businessman. I had married a workaholic, who was actually in love with his business. Even* Fortune *magazine said, "Harry runs the cooking line like the Radio City Rockettes."*

Indeed, nothing had changed. He still wasn't there in the early morning when I woke and wanted to cuddle. He was at work. And he still didn't roll back into the house until 3:00 A.M., after I was asleep. I would have to settle into his comfort level, not mine.

I knew he loved me deeply, but you can't change a man, especially a man who loves work. Loves the recognition. Loves solving problems. Loves pleasing each and every guest. *Hey baby, remember me? I'm alone here in this big house. Many couples get derailed with this cyclonic mixture of romance and business.*

"THERE'S A DIVINITY THAT SHAPES OUR ENDS"

—Hamlet

Getting back to your own kitchen after being away can be an incredibly warm experience. *I remembered the $6,000 baked apples in the early days, and how warm they made the kitchens feel. The boys never forgot that delicious aroma. It was their childhood.* But this kitchen didn't have those smells. It was an empty nest. The boys were away and Harry was away at the stores, making sure they were "lookin' just as fine as a 'gentleman's handkerchief drawer.'" I had been away for ten years, building up our business on the East Coast and being Cardinali. Much had changed. I wanted to be challenged again by the creativity I saw in Chicago.

In Chicago, the foods were so new. When I left, the restaurants were just starting to be on the cutting edge. With all the diversity of the people and their cultures, it was a wealth of "new." Just like New York, it was a culinary explosion! The new young chefs were mixing it all up. Alice Waters in Berkeley was taking restaurant cooking to new heights. I was determined to learn all the new foods.

LEARNING THE NEW FOODS.

A new culture was afoot. People dined out every night and it was stylish. New foods were in the markets. New restaurants were popping up all over with chefs who were suddenly the new stars. The new foods of the '80s were fascinating and mysterious. Wild mesclun greens, 100-point tomatoes, exotic funghi, balsamic vinegars, verjuice, goat cheese, and crème fraîche. People in the market (including me) were scratching their heads. We would look at each other hoping for a clue.

Young women chefs were emerging in a big way, but rather silently. The kudos were going to the boy-chefs, as usual. *I was used to that in the design business.* Talking about food as if it were fashion was de rigeur. It was the new American "thing" to act like you knew all about these new foods, intimately.

For those who wanted to learn, cooking classes were abundant. If you had money to burn, you could learn directly from a famous chef. Stores like Williams-Sonoma and Crate & Barrel fed the "yuppie" foodies' new lifestyle. They bought everything related to cooking to show off their newfound skills. They bought the professional-sized kitchen ranges and oversized refrigerators with glass doors for their own kitchens, and hired private chefs to cook for them. Dining was sexy! It was indeed an exciting time, except that I wanted to slow down, gain a little weight, and cook my heart out. The kitchen was a good, warm place for me to be, to get my peripheral senses stirred up. Even those who don't cook say it's the sexiest way to spend a lonely hour. Men and women both. Nothing heals like cooking.

THE NEW FOODS, CIRCA 1984

CRÈME FRAÎCHE

We've had sour cream in this country for years, but when crème fraîche came over from France, sour cream had to take the backseat. It became our joke around the house when Harry would always ask, of any new recipe I was trying, "But does it have crème fraîche in it?" His dry wit in place. It did add an interesting flavor, and whenever a food needed softening, or a little extra subtle tang, I learned to add a spoon or two of crème fraîche.

It's a thick, rich, and voluptuous cream similar to the English Devonshire cream. They both resemble a light sour cream. Crème fraîche is used by every new chef around the country for all kinds of cooking, baking, and plating. Spoon it over berries. Add a dollop to scrambled eggs while they're cooking. Mix it with Dijon mustard for a sandwich, or to top steamed asparagus. Add it to any sauce that asks for heavy cream, for a tiny bit of tartness. It's terribly expensive to buy, but easy to make.

CRÈME FRAÎCHE

MIX 4 CUPS OF HEAVY CREAM WITH 4 TABLESPOONS BUTTERMILK. ❧ COVER AND KEEP IN A WARM PLACE FOR 24 HOURS (NOT DRAFTY OR AIR CONDITIONED — FIND A CUPBOARD AND COVER SNUGLY WITH A TOWEL). ❧ REFRIGERATE FOR AT LEAST 6 HOURS BEFORE USING.

BALSAMIC VINEGAR:
WHY IS IT SO EXPENSIVE AND WHAT'S THE BIG DEAL?

Balsamic is made from white Trebbiano grapes, and then stored in the family's attic in big juniper barrels. Then, the family begins taking a series of fifteen-year vacations. When they come back, they put whatever is left in the barrel into another barrel. Then they go away again for another fifteen years. Sixty years later they make the last transfer. Then they wait until the seventy fifth year when there remains just a tiny little bit. Nectar from the gods. A northern Italian treasure with a glorious flavor. The older the balsamic, the more it costs. Of course, there is a simpler, faster version. Otherwise, no restaurant could afford it and there wouldn't be enough to keep up with the demand.

EDIBLE FLOWERS

Flowers on food are blooming. Being used simply to beautify a plate presentation. But eating flowers can be hazardous to your health…if they're sprayed. Women try them. Men push them aside. Nasturtium, borage, pansies, zucchini flowers, chive flowers, and lavender. All expensive. Frankly, I don't covet them. But if you do, use only the ones sold for food preparation or from your garden, not those sold from a florist's stand.

CHÈVRE (GOAT CHEESE)

The versatile tangy cheese derived from goat's milk is called "chev" (Don't pronounce the "re.") The French regions of Burgundy, Cognac, and Dordogne originally produced this delectable cheese. Now, we're producing our very own chèvre in Sonoma County because of Laura Chenel. Laura is a very smart young lady who had more goats than she knew what to do with, so she hotfooted it to France to learn. *I respect her so much for taking the time to learn such an unusual craft. She pursued her dream and went the limit to learn. You can't wing it. Now, she is the largest and youngest cheese producer in America. Good for her.*

Goat cheese changed the American sandwich, as we knew it. When goat cheese came of age, mayonnaise took a backseat for a while.

And it gave salads a new taste. Now, vinaigrettes made more sense. We could replace the old creamy, fatty dressings (which literally laid on top of the lettuce leaves like a clod).

Could there be anything better than goat cheese, French bread, and grapes after a meal?

Understanding Camembert

Did you ever find yourself staring down at a lot of wonderful smelly cheeses? "Should I buy the Brie or the Camembert? What is the difference?"

Well, not too much. Brie was the first, dating back to the fifteenth century. It was proclaimed "King of Cheese" by the legendary gourmand Tallyrand, after the Battle of Waterloo. Shelf life is about three weeks, so be sure it has a mellow, custardy consistency when you buy it. Store soft cheeses like Brie in the veggie drawer alongside a head of lettuce (this provides needed humidity) and take it out of the fridge at least an hour before you plan to serve it.

Wild Mushrooms

What are chanterelles, morels, and *pleurotes?* They are the earthy but elegant wild mushrooms of France. The price can be daunting, but think of it as a pound of feathers…. Mushrooms weigh very little, so that when you buy a few, the price is not so bad. Choose a few different varieties and mix them up. They add such organic beauty to any dish. The one crucial thing I learned was never to soak or wash them in water. Use a little soft, wet mushroom brush to brush them clean, one at a time in your hand. Rinse the brush after each brushing. That's all you need to do. Cut off the stems and discard the woody stems, or use them for soup. Always sauté sliced mushrooms in a wide pan and give them plenty of room, so they can get nicely brown and bleed off their excess moisture. Oh, and don't use salt while cooking or they will purge even more water. Salt only at the end. Use just a bit of olive oil in a large pan, otherwise they'll "stew," which you *do not* want.

Parmigiano-Reggiano and Pecorino Romano

Parmigiano-Reggiano is made in northern Italy of cow's milk. Pecorino is from southern Italy and made from sheep's milk. Pecorino is the saltier of the two, and wonderful to use with bitter greens and pasta.

"She's Back"

I'm afraid this was the centerpiece of conversation in our town. Everyone wanted to see who I was and how Harry and I "were" together. We were invited out like a new couple for all to see. I could sense the game that was being played, but I weathered it. I was home now, and standing on firm ground. Ladies, look out! Harry was, of course, amused. Not two weeks had passed when Harry was dragging me to see another location. *Here I thought we might slow it up a bit and do the things we had never made the time to do before. Like take a cruise somewhere, learn to play golf together, go to the movies, hold hands, dress down on a Saturday afternoon, go window-shopping. We hadn't even gotten that far when we were off to see the next one....*

But I couldn't argue, the new location was glorious! The minute I saw it, I knew I was entering another level. It couldn't be anything but the Hamlet Gardens. It was a romantic space and visually beautiful. Harry was very enthusiastic.

Everyone always thought it was me who kept spawning new locations, when in fact, I would have been just as happy and content to stay in my own kitchen and put on a few pounds.

"Hamlet Gardens? What is that?" Harry asked.

"I don't know yet." I walked around slowly to see what I could feel.

There was softness and a romantic informality. The open courtyard would need a huge dome, thirty feet high. There would have to be a tree. An important tree right in the middle under the glass dome. I was thinking out loud.

"Harry, this room could be this and that room could be that. The bar would be here. It could even have a bar menu, with its own little kitchen. The main kitchen would be over there...."

"Two kitchens?" Harry asked. "That's going to be complicated, and too expensive to staff."

"We could do pizzas and cappuccino in the bar, and install a telephone to the kitchen," I said.

Harry rolled his eyes. "But what's on the menu?"

"What's on the menu?" I froze. It reminded me of when he had first asked me, "Marilyn, are you sure you can cook?"

Now that I understood the new foods, we were able to start thinking about the menu for the Gardens. It was going to be a good one. We did build the two kitchens: one off the bar and one main kitchen. The informal bar menu made it possible to offer everyone's favorite foods: hamburger, pizza, and cappuccino. The main kitchen would offer all the new, sophisticated, and creative foods we were learning. And what a location this was, with movie theaters all around.

The budget was steep: $4 million. We acid-washed the red brick interior to a soft, variegated peach tone, all faded and pale. For the bar floor, we chose clay tiles dotted with glazed sapphire and emerald corners. Gleaming copper clad the cooking bar, and spit grout ceiling boards created the warmest French country look. The whole effect was right out of the South of France. The glass dome was installed thirty feet up in the center atrium, and it was ready for a wonderful tree. We chose a very young, fourteen-foot ficus. It was too tall to go through the door, so we laid it on its side and dragged it in by rope, very carefully, like a baby calf, and planted it under the glass dome.

"You have twenty more feet to grow and we will take good care of you," I told the tree.

You may think it odd to talk to a tree, but later on I'll tell you what it all meant to me, and to the tree.

I pinched myself over and over remembering how we opened the first Hamlet in 1950 with a mere $3,500. And yet, this was still risky business. Even though our public had loved us in the hamburger business for all these years, there was no guarantee they would accept this change of price-point and new milieu. But, I was a gambler (with a nervous stomach). Harry was a gambler with kind of quiet that could make you quake. There was a lot of money going into this place, and who could know?

When it was finished, it was absolutely extraordinarily beautiful!

It was the Jewel in our Crown.

ROCK SHRIMP AND
FUSILLI ADRIATIC

SERVES 4

You will think you are eating something that was pulled from the Adriatic just five minutes before. I like to serve this with a simple bruschetta: just a toasted piece of rustic bread rubbed with a cut clove of garlic.

- ꙮ BRING A VERY LARGE POT OF SALTED WATER TO THE BOIL FOR COOKING THE FUSILLI.

- ꙮ COOK FOR ABOUT 8 MINUTES, OR UNTIL SOFT (YOU DO NOT WANT THE PASTA AL DENTE FOR THIS DISH):

  1 POUND FUSILLI PASTA

- ꙮ DRAIN WELL AND TURN OUT INTO A LARGE, WARMED MIXING BOWL. WHILE THE PASTA IS BOILING, BRING TO A VERY SLOW SIMMER (SMALL BUBBLES) IN A SAUCEPAN:

  1 1/2 CUPS FISH STOCK

- ꙮ ADD AND SIMMER FOR 30 TO 45 SECONDS ONLY, UNTIL BARELY OPAQUE. (DO NOT OVERCOOK!):

  10 OUNCES SHELLED ROCK SHRIMP

  10 OUNCES SCALLOPS, HALVED CROSSWISE

- ꙮ WITH A SLOTTED SPOON, TRANSFER THE SEAFOOD TO THE BOWL OF PASTA. IMMEDIATELY ADD:

  1/3 CUP FRESH LEMON JUICE

  2/3 CUP EXTRA VIRGIN OLIVE OIL

  1/2 TO 3/4 TEASPOON KOSHER SALT

  1/4 TEASPOON FRESHLY GROUND BLACK PEPPER

continued   Rock Shrimp and Fusilli Adriatic

꩜ TOSS QUICKLY AND THOROUGHLY, GETTING THE OLIVE OIL
AND JUICES WELL DISTRIBUTED THROUGH THE PASTA.
IMMEDIATELY TRANSFER TO WARMED PLATES FOR SERVING AND
TOP EVENLY WITH:

   1 CUP FIRMLY PACKED ARUGULA LEAVES (ABOUT 1 OUNCE),
   CUT INTO WIDE JULIENNE

TOMATO SOUP WITH ORANGE JUICE KISSED WITH ANGOSTURA BITTERS

First make the ceviche garnish, so the little bundles are ready.

꩜ IN A GLASS BOWL, COMBINE:

   $^1/_2$ POUND FROZEN FILLET OF SOLE, CHOPPED IN SMALL PIECES

   JUICE OF 2 LEMONS

   JUICE OF 2 ORANGES

   JUICE OF 1 LIME

   2 TABLESPOONS FINELY MINCED RED ONION

꩜ COVER WITH PLASTIC WRAP AND REFRIGERATE FOR
30 MINUTES, NOT MORE.

꩜ THEN MIX TOGETHER IN A SAUCEPAN:

   2 CUPS LOW-FAT CHICKEN BROTH

   2 CUPS TOMATO JUICE

   2 CUPS FRESHLY SQUEEZED ORANGE JUICE

continued   Tomato Soup with Orange Juice Kissed with Angostura bitters

A TINY DROP OF ANGOSTURA BITTERS

☙ HEAT THE SOUP GENTLY AND PREHEAT THE BROILER.

☙ TOAST UNTIL PALE GOLDEN:

THIN SLICES OF BAGUETTE BREAD

☙ LADLE THE SOUP INTO BOWLS, FLOAT A SLICE OF BAGUETTE
IN THE CENTER, AND PINCH A LITTLE BIT OF THE CEVICHE
ON TOP OF EACH BAGUETTE (PINCHING HELPS HOLD THE
FISH TOGETHER).

"THERE IS NO VIRTUE LIKE NECESSITY"

—Richard II

My own kitchen at home was a joke. We had never taken the time or the money to improve that most important room. Our money was always being spent on new locations. More than once, we'd had to put our home on the block, *as you know,* but we always got it back.

Now it was time. If we were going to have a swell new restaurant with a completely different menu, one that depended on a real "chef," we were going to have to update our own kitchen at home. The kitchen in the new Gardens hadn't yet been constructed, leaving our kitchen at home a terrible little place to do research and development for the new menu. Finally, Harry agreed to invest in an upgraded kitchen at home. *It was also comforting that this kind of R&D was a write-off.*

We started with three little boxes typical of an older home: the breakfast room, the kitchen, and the laundry room. All the walls came down to make one huge room.

We installed a white enameled French fireplace between two white steel St. Charles vertical cupboards (mixing the periods, yes). The ceiling was copper-paneled, the walls, white Mylar. The floors were white Italian tiles. A huge center island dominated, with white Corian and three stainless-steel pendant lamps overhead. Two refrigerators and one freezer were built in, with television and VCR overhead (replete with instructional cooking tapes). A greenhouse above the sink was planted with herbs. And the final touch: a Biedermeier sofa adjacent to the fireplace with a wonderfully luminous "Lichtenstein" painting over it. If you can imagine the energy bouncing off the illuminated reflections: the roaring fireplace and the copper ceiling. Such a new room in this old house was dazzling!

This was where we proudly brought our first *real* chef and his sous chef to do the research and development for our new Hamlet Gardens. Robert Van Houten would be the chef, and Michel, his sous. Fortunately, they were both soft-spoken and generous, which made the hours very peaceful. I was thrilled to watch their amazing ease and sense of order. It was a new life for me at home.

A bonus: It turned out to be a perfect room for a black-tie event, which we hosted for PBS. A formal party, in the kitchen, where all the guests dressed to the hilt and helped themselves around the magnificent center island buffet. It was so different! They loved it! Julia Child among them. It was in honor of her.

The new "Jewel in our Crown" sparked the interest of a Harvard MBA graduate, who decided that he might like to "own" our "chain of restaurants." *By this time, there were twenty-three. With the addition of the Gardens and some of the real estate we had amassed over the years, he was moved to feel very romantic about us. He wanted to buy our business!* Ignoring him and his offer, we went to work on yet another new location and a new concept.

Kay O'Krand

Julia Child
Reception

Hosted by KCET, Marilyn & Harry Lewis and The American Institute of Wine & Food
Butler Passed
Pan Seared Ginger Prawns Flamed with Sake & Lime
Blue Corn Blinis Topped with California Golden Caviar

Counter Top Buffet Supper
Nicoise Salad Compose with Fresh Grilled Tuna

Pot Au Feu featuring Pot of Beef Brisket simmered with Baby Carrots, Belgian Endive, Pearl Onions, & Red Rose Potatoes served Brasserie style accompanied by Poached Chicken and Sausage with

Pot Au Feu Broth and Homemade Dumplings

Rustic Breads—Onion, Potato, Pumpernickel with Whipped Butter

Finale

Lace Cookies Cornicopias filled with Vanilla Bean Ice Cream & drizzled with Three Sauces: Chocolate, Caramel, Raspberry

Fresh Fruits of the Season with Creme Anglaise

Coffee Bar

Photo by Mitzi Trumbo.

IMAGINE CREATING A SUMPTUOUS BUFFET FOR A PARTY HONORING JULIA CHILD! I PRACTICED BRISKET AND POT-AU-FEU UNTIL I ALMOST GOT IT RIGHT. SHE THOUGHT IT WAS WONDERFUL.

"MARILYN, ARE YOU SURE YOU CAN COOK?" HE ASKED

An old bank building came up, on the corner of Wilshire and Doheny at the eastern entrance of Beverly Hills. A very important corner, two blocks from the Academy Awards Arts and Science Building. One block from the Writers Guild. Two blocks from the International Creative Management Agency (ICM). A powerhouse movie industry corner. This site had never actually gone on the market. Instead, it was "brought to us privately" (like having "the first look" at a script, as an actor).

Harry and I stood in this 100-foot-long rectangular space. It had been a bank. But to me, it was a food hall! I looked up to note the ceiling height. Thirty feet. Immediately, I was struck with the concept.

It had to be "Kate Mantilini Steak House—open all night!"

Harry did a double take. "What is that?" he asked.

"Kate Mantilini," I said, "Kate was my Uncle Rob's mistress in the '40s…."

"We've been married over thirty years and I never heard you mention this?" He said.

"I just thought of it this minute. It just hit me. The bones of the space and this unbelievable corner just scream out Kate Mantilini." My voice trailed off as I explained. "The name of a very strong woman, who was way before her time. I guess she's been with me always, I just didn't get the message until now."

"No one will be able to spell it. How *do* you spell it?" he implored.

"M-A-N-T-I-L-I-N-I. Don't worry about it," I said. "It's perfect." *I just knew it.*

Kate Mantilini's (almost all-night) Steak House opened on St. Patrick's Day 1987. We won the Progressive Architectural Award for the best in avant-garde design. The *New York Times* gave it a full page.

The story of Kate was repeated by so many people that it changed constantly. Like playing the game "Telephone" when you're a kid: You sit in a row and everyone whispers the same secret in the next person's ear, and when it finally gets to the last person, it's a completely different story. "Kate" went from being my Uncle Rob's mistress to my grandfather's mistress who ran a brothel. My mother begged me to stop giving out the story as it was "hurting the family's reputation."

"How could you name such a gorgeous place after such a terrible woman?" she asked.

"Please stop, Mother, give it a rest. After all these years, who cares? It's perfect, and besides, everyone loves hearing about her."

The menu was fixed in my mind, just like the name and the style. Every new restaurant was serving food with commas. Food was described with so many ingredients that they had to be listed with comma after comma after comma. John Dory (the new *wunder*-fish) was always first in a long line of fish specials. And there were all the really new foods, which everyone had to try (whether they were good or not). I thought the fish movement was over the top, just like the pasta craze, I thought. Enough already! We had a restaurant (Hamlet Gardens) that explored the hot new trends. Now we needed to go back to basics.

Maybe basic food is what I know best, but instinctively I longed for some good old-fashioned comfort food. Somewhere out there were hungry people looking for great food like meatloaf, pork chops, crab cakes, sand dabs, mashed potatoes, and hot fudge sundaes with lots of whipped cream and sugar-glazed nuts. All these would be on Kate's menu. Were we out of step? Well, maybe. But not for long. The budget here was, again, almost $4 million, and again my stomach hurt and Harry got quieter. Our routine. And the Harvard MBA got even *more* romantic.

Our son David called from Vienna. *He had spinal meningitis.* We packed so fast and flew there "with no plane." Twice a day we visited the hospital for six long freezing-cold weeks, and every day we prayed. That he made it and was released from the hospital was a miracle answered through our prayers. Until he could be on his own again, we stayed with him, in Vienna.

David was eventually able to return to his job at the United Nations, where he headed up the language department at a very large immigration camp called

Before leaving Vienna, Harry felt he had to warn me, once again, not to be looking around for people to bring back to America. It was fine to collect recipes, *but not people*. (Harry wasn't amused by my recruiting habits, since travel expenses and housing were a serious cost.)

There was a young, well-groomed Austrian cook who laid the exquisite breakfast table every morning at the Hotel Imperial, where we were staying. I watched his every move and was convinced he would make a solid contribution to our new Gardens. I felt we should talk with him, and see if he had any interest. Harry, of course, held his head in his hands, with that "here she goes again" look. The man's name was Walter (pronounced "Valter"), and he did indeed want to come to America. In fact, he was thrilled at the opportunity. He would show us how to do Wiener Schnitzel and pickled vegetables.

He was so well groomed. Not a hair out of place. So respectful, he almost curtsied when he greeted you. We arranged for everything, and he came over with dispatch. Three months later, he had long unkempt hair and came to work needing a shave. When I asked, "What happened to the wonderfully groomed young man who came here from Vienna?" He answered, "But I'm in America now." He went back home with the same dispatch.

Traiskirchen, teaching English as a second language.

As soon as we got home, David called from Vienna to tell us that the immigration business was all but dried up since the Iron Curtain had lifted. He felt he'd "like to take a chance and join the family business."

"But what would you do?" I asked.

"Well, Mom, since I've been in Europe for so many years, and I really like cooking quite a bit...."

He came home.

Hamburger Hamlets Sold for $33.1 Million

"Hamburger Hamlets, the Southern California restaurant chain that began as a Sunset Strip takeout stand equipped with a hot plate *(ill-described, I would say)*, has agreed to be acquired by a New York investment firm for about $33.1 million, it was announced Tuesday.

"Founders Harry and Marilyn Lewis will remain as consultants for five years and, after the transaction is completed, will buy back the chain's trendy Kate Mantilini restaurant in Beverly Hills for an undisclosed amount. Weatherly Private Capital, Inc., will pay $9.20 for each of Hamburger Hamlets' 3.6 million outstanding common shares, 70% of which are held by the Lewises.

'We got a very good offer,' said Harry Lewis, president of the chain. 'They intend to keep it exactly the same, and we're staying on to see that it is kept that way.'

'None of the 1,600 Hamburger Hamlets employees will be laid off, he said.' *This was paramount to us.*

"In over-the-counter trading Tuesday, Hamburger Hamlet's shares closed at $7.50, up $1.

"Lewis hinted that Weatherly might expand the Sherman Oaks-based chain, which has twenty-four restaurants in Southern California, Chicago, and the Washington, D.C. area. But officials at Weatherly were noncommittal.

"Although Hamburger Hamlets sold stock to the public in 1969, the Lewises have retained tight control of company ownership and operations. Marilyn Lewis, for instance, is in charge of developing menus and interior design. She also serves as Chairman."

Jesus Sanchez—*Los Angeles Times*

"No Profit Grows
Where No Pleasure Is Taken"

—The Taming of the Shrew

Our son David and I tried to stop the sale from happening, but at that point Harry wanted it more than anything. It was a lot of money being offered, and he suddenly felt tired for the first time in thirty-eight years. David and I felt that we had a very strong customer base. He was enjoying his position watching over the cooking line, and we both felt that we should keep the company in the family. Harry insisted we sell. It was a lot of money and he felt good about it.

But I sensed he could not be happy away from his live daily "show." He needed somewhere to go each day, and needed to see his audience (his customers). Solving problems seemed to give him a reason for living.

I did insist, successfully, that we have the right to buy back either the Hamlet Gardens or Kate Mantilini.

You'd think a man who just received over $33 million for his business would be dancing on air. Well, it didn't work out that way. Harry was so depressed he couldn't smile, he couldn't eat, and he couldn't sleep. The very idea that he'd sold his baby—his life—away to somebody else, was unbelievable to him. I would think this syndrome is fairly common, but there are trade-offs, aren't there? After having worked for thirty-eight years...wouldn't receiving all that money be something wonderful in exchange? The first question out of everyone's mouth was "Are you happy you sold?"

He would inevitably turn sad, and respond, "No," which shocked everyone who heard it.

"You're kidding!" They would say.

"No, I'm not kidding. Marilyn is happy about it, but I'm not," Harry would reply.

But it was you, Harry, who wanted to sell, not me! I was only happy that we had the option to buy back Kate Mantilini. That we'd have a place for the family now that David was home.

I thought this depression Harry was feeling would go away in time. That it was natural to have these feelings. We've talked to quite a few people who sold their businesses, and they all said that there is that kind of sorrow for a short time. But with Harry it never went away.

Howard W. Koch would invite him to the Paramount studio commissary for lunch, and try to cheer him up. We all tried. There was nothing I could say to him that helped. Nothing. It was time for celebration, but there was none.

Our dear friend, Fred Hayman, creator of Giorgio Perfume, sold his company to Avon for millions. He smartly retained the right to keep his famous shop on Rodeo Drive in Beverly Hills, which was renamed Fred Hayman's. Like Harry, Fred is a people person, an elegant man who still wanted to oversee the European collections with his wonderful wife, Betty, and have a say in all matters. It gave him his base.

Harry listened and we did buy back Kate Mantilini, which telephone operators and customers calling for the number had no trouble spelling. *We bought back Kate Mantilini, that was good, and the MBA Harvard graduate got the Gardens, that was sad.*

It was then one year old. Now, I thought, we had a strong place for our son David to learn to be an executive chef. Then, Adam called. *Adam wanted to be in the family business too.* We were down to one restaurant. What to do?

How many executive sons can you have in one business? He agreed to start on the floor as a waiter, just as David had started as a prep man in the kitchen. That was fine, but it was not working internally, as the other waiters felt uncomfortable having the owner's son on the floor with them. We had to find his métier, where he excelled (and where we could afford to put him). He was a stockbroker, about ready to get unmarried, and living in Minneapolis. He had four children. This would really be starting over for him, and all kinds of new problems for us. One restaurant cannot afford to support so many. But when it's your family, you have to let them in.

Adam was good at figures and he understood bottom lines, so without hesitation, up to the office he went.

While David was holding down the kitchen and the cooking line, Adam was developing computer programs on food costs and labor costs. He had the benefit of learning how to solve all the day-to-day problems from his father, an expert. He had me to go through all the communication issues with: writing the orientation manuals, the art of writing a memo to the employees, the art of speaking with employees, the art of writing to a customer—the art... the art.... *I was teaching the American University course: "Owning your Own Business, An American Dream," all over again.... But this time, instead of a room full of strangers it was a class of two, our sons. It was a thrill. Our sons were back with us and now we, Harry and I, could afford to get just a little tired. Or so I thought.*

David had to learn everything. He had to learn how to be an executive chef from the get-go. I became his Julia Child. We went to cooking classes together. We watched videos. We cooked together. We argued. He sulked. We always made up, through food.

BOTH OF OUR SONS,
WITH HARRY.

I taught David how a chef had to be a perfectionist, and watch every little thing, even a hard-boiled egg: "If a hard-boiled egg has a dark circle around the yolk," I told him, "I know it's been cooked incorrectly."

(I just can't stop myself from examining every egg on a Tuna Nicoise, even in other people's restaurants. I want to know how careful that kitchen is.)

And I love M.F.K. Fisher's description of a perfectly cooked hard-boiled egg.

"You mean you watch *an egg,* too?" David asked.

"Yes, I watch an egg, too," I answered. "It's called quality control."

COOKING THE PERFECT HARD-BOILED EGG

- ꙮ GENTLY PLACE EGGS IN AN EMPTY POT.
- ꙮ COVER WITH COLD WATER. ADD:

  1 TABLESPOON SALT OR A CAPFUL OF PLAIN VINEGAR

- ꙮ COVER. BRING TO A BOIL, STANDING BY.
- ꙮ AT THE FIRST SIGN OF THE BOIL, TURN OFF THE HEAT AND COVER.
- ꙮ LET STAND FOR 12 MINUTES.
- ꙮ THEN *immediately* RUN UNDER COLD WATER TO STOP THE COOKING.
- ꙮ CRACK AND REMOVE SHELL (EASILY).

You will have a perfectly cooked egg with no black ring around it and a wonderful texture to the yolk.

"Presume Not
That I Am the Thing I Was"

—Henry IV, Part Two

Lewis Cooks Up 2 Projects To Launch Production Firm

"Former Hamburger Hamlets restaurant chain co-owner Marilyn Lewis, four weeks since hanging out her shingle in business as Marilyn Lewis Entertainment Enterprises, has received 28 script submissions. It's tempting, Lewis acknowledges, to use her own money to finance her productions, but vows 'absolutely not' to do that until MLEE 'turns its first two projects.' With those initial two, she wants to be known as a new indie, bringing to the table unique concepts and style. The first 'let's have lunch' Lewis attended turned out to have an $8 Mil lunch price tag, if she went along with all the ideas laid across the table. She wasn't interested. The emphasis will be on the optioning of literary properties, and she envisions the company as being in both features and TV. The restaurant business, she says, is 'a live show daily,' and so this is a natural extension of what she's been doing since opening the first Hamburger Hamlet. Lewis considers that, in essence, she's never been out of show business since that time, especially given her second career as a designer, under the name of Cardinali. Lewis is in the process of assembling a staff which will include development execs. She's operating out of an office next to Kate Mantilini on Wilshire Blvd., the one restaurant she and her husband retain.

"Harry Lewis is not involved in MLEE but if a good acting role comes available in one of the new company's projects, she says, he'll get every consideration for the part."

—Morrie Gelman, *Variety*

No sooner had *Variety* announced my debut into the movie biz in seventy-five-point banner headlines, the first wave of lunches began. Each lunch I took began and ended with a pitch for money: bridge money, seed money, production money, first-tier money, *any money*. The next wave came with writers and their scripts. These lunches were filled with endless lists of interested studios and stars who wanted to be attached to the project (mostly imaginary). It was the game and everyone played it, except the major players. Only when you become a "player" does all this stop.

I was always in production with some extravaganza or another. Opening one restaurant after another required vision, creativity, and purpose. It was certainly a live show daily, the restaurant business, just as I'd said. Once the press shouted out the story of the big sale, everyone looking for money or financing for their movie came running to meet me. To have lunch with me. I was really not attracted to the deals or the material. Then one day, a friend I respected, Joan Agajanian Quinn, suggested that I get involved in the life of Andy Warhol.

Andy Warhol was a solid project. It was *Superstar: The Life and Times of Andy Warhol,* and I would be executive producer. It is well known in the industry that you should never use your own money. I solemnly swore not to do it. Harry warned me, and elder statesman/board member Howard W. Koch warned me. I got caught and did it anyway. *How could you lose? I reasoned.*

Academy Award winner Chuck Workman directed, and nothing was spared to make it a big screen presence.

Superstar: The Life and Times of Andy Warhol. A definitive documentary on his life. Crazy as he was, he had appeal. It seemed to me that we were in a blue chip area: Andy Warhol was an icon like Marilyn Monroe, who had universal appeal and would last forever. I liked that. Trends and fads never interested me. I always had to keep my ear to the ground. I couldn't exactly dismiss trends, but I always managed to stay close to the classics. Things people felt the most comfortable eating, wearing, watching. Updated, of course, but if it had a bubble attached to it, I wasn't interested.

MARILYN LEWIS ENTERTAINMENT LTD. PRESENTS
A FILM BY CHUCK WORKMAN

THE LIFE AND TIMES OF ANDY WARHOL

MARILYN LEWIS ENTERTAINMENT LTD. PRESENTS A FILM BY CHUCK WORKMAN SUPERSTAR
EXECUTIVE PRODUCER MARILYN LEWIS CO-EXECUTIVE PRODUCER PETER ENGLISH NELSON
PRODUCTION EXECUTIVE STEPHEN J. KERN DIRECTOR OF PHOTOGRAPHY BURLEIGH WARTES
LINE PRODUCER JAMES CADY ASSOCIATE PRODUCER LARRY GREEN
WRITTEN, PRODUCED AND DIRECTED BY CHUCK WORKMAN
© 1990, MARILYN LEWIS ENTERTAINMENT LTD.

What I wasn't aware of were the vultures. The foreign distributor who would follow you to all the film festivals begging for the opportunity to distribute your wonderful film. I fell prey to their passion and sensibility, and I got burned. Yes! Once you've signed, he collects all the money and makes all the sales and then politely declares bankruptcy a year later, when all the hoop-de-la is over. Once you've sold your product and done the circuit and the marketing, you can't come back with a stale old theme. *Seen that, done that, been there.* "Show me something new!" You can't remarket the same product with too much excitement, once someone has used up your time. The shelf life is short.

Then there's the American distributor. He follows you too. He has warmth and passion and sensibility for your film. He can be trusted. Once you sign, he sells all the ancillary rights to video, to Bravo, to PBS, to Education. Takes the money and before you get your share, he very politely declares bankruptcy. So far, you haven't seen a dime.

Later, in seven long years, you can start over. You get another chance to peddle it. Isn't that a nice word: "peddle." You can generate new interest and hope a caller comes again.

Even the T-shirts we did were knocked off and we had to sue. We won, but winning meant nothing. It was uncomfortable being in a business where you lose your "say," your power, to so many others.

At least in your own business, you can blame yourself if things go wrong, and make some "corrections," as the stockmarket guys say. You can get a fresh start—but not in the movie business. There are too many people involved. Too many subjective decisions being made. Too much politic-playing. Too much nepotism. *Not to say that nepotism is a bad thing. It's actually a good thing. I did it with my own family. But in the movie business, when you're an outsider, you're an outsider.*

I was still paying to store the Warhol film every month, waiting for the next seven-year cycle. But then what do you know? The Angel of Distribution arrived and Winstar acquired the film until the year 2010! *My angels always seem to come through when I need them most.*

Reading books, looking for a possible movie, or movie of the week, I discovered Ayn Rand on Connie Martinson's TV show *Talking Books.* A woman named Barbara Branden had written a best-seller called *The Passion of Ayn Rand.* I called Connie the next day, who led me to Barbara Branden, and I optioned the book. We chose a particular segment of the book that focused on Ayn's torrid May-December love affair with twenty-year-old Nathaniel Branden, the ex-husband of the author.

Ayn Rand was the author of *The Fountainhead, Atlas Shrugged,* and *We the Living.* Compulsory college reading. Important. Over the years, her works sold second to the Bible. So important were her views on capitalism, government, and collectivism, they have been studied by presidents and scholars the world over. Every word by her regarding a free society was coveted by Iron Curtain immigrants thirsty for the ideas she espoused. Every educated American man wanted to be like her Howard Roarke *(The Fountainhead)* or John Gault *(Atlas).*

I remember Harry taking me by our little Hamlet one night, while I was pregnant with our first son. He wanted me to see the crowds out on the sidewalk, the overflow of popularity our restaurant had. It scared me. I thought it was the bubble and it was sure to burst. I convinced him to close earlier in order to attract the serious diner and lose the sidewalk overflow.

"That's a helluva lot of revenue to lose, Marilyn," he said. "It will be better for us in the long run," I answered. And it was. Greedy makes you needy, I think.

For eight years, I made the rounds to top producers and heads of studios pitching my Ayn Rand project. This was very hard for me, as I am not a "pitcher." It scared me that the shyness would return. These very important people opened their doors. They all knew and respected me, so gaining entry to them was easy. What I could not seem to do was to sway their opinions about her, Ayn Rand. Each one of them independently said things like "I wouldn't touch her with a ten-foot pole."

"But why?"

"Because I hate her politics," was the common response.

"What politics?"

"McCarthyism!"

"She didn't believe in McCarthyism! She was against Communist infiltration into her beloved, adopted America! Her beliefs were based on her own experience, when the Bolsheviks disrupted her family's life, her education, and her roots! This is where she was coming from; it wasn't McCarthyism! She was using the platform to be heard. She was not meanspirited! She had suffered from the age of twelve at the hands of the Bolsheviks and their insurgence. She knew it firsthand."

I got nowhere.

But, to quote her exactly: An acquaintance of Ayn congratulated her on her courage in agreeing to testify before the House Un-American Activities Committee, and she replied, "I'm not brave enough to be a coward. I see the consequences too clearly."

Among the "friendly witnesses" were Ayn Rand, Adolphe Menjou, Ronald Reagan, Robert Taylor, and Gary Cooper. Many of these people were told tacitly or openly that cooperation with the committee would be professionally damaging to them. (Mr. Menjou found fewer and fewer jobs, Mr. Cooper's stardom never faltered, and Ronald Reagan became the fortieth president of the United States.)

If someone important was interested in my Rand project, it tended to last seventeen minutes, until they heard the same protests I did. Every once in a while, I would think of someone new to bring it to. Until one day at Kate Mantilini, my own restaurant, I spied a man with a perfectly contoured white goatee, wearing a ski sweater and waiting for a table.

I don't know why I was drawn to him but it was a bull's eye!

I went up to him and asked point-blank, "What is your name? I've seen you here so often and I feel I should know you."

"Irwin Meyer," he answered, somewhat amused.

"Are you in the business?"

He smiled and nodded.

"Good, I want to talk to you about a project I own. When can we…?" I asked.

"If you can get me a table, how about now?" He offered.

"You bet I can!"

When I told him it was Ayn Rand, he got so excited, he couldn't eat.

Bull's eye.

The author of *The Passion of Ayn Rand*, Barbara Branden, is an interesting woman. She originally gave me the project because she believed in my passion. It was personal for her. Barbara was in the story from the beginning. When she and her first husband, Nathaniel, were young lovers and students at UCLA, they discovered they both loved the novel *The Fountainhead* and Ayn Rand's philosophies. They had the serendipitous fortune to meet Ayn and be invited to her home, and this became the matrix of their relationship.

To sit at her feet, listening until all hours of the night, was the most erotic adventure to both of them. She loved their young, active minds, and invited them often. Ayn was the matron of honor at their wedding. Later, Ayn chose Nathaniel as her lover, which was consistent with her ideas on sexual freedom. Who better than Barbara to write this story?

Barbara wrote a 442-page tome in 1986, which stayed on the *New York Times* best-seller list for seven weeks. It was a masterpiece.

I made a partnership deal with Irwin.

Two years passed.

Nothing much was happening.

One day I heard Diane Keaton was interested.

Then I heard we were having a script written.

Then I heard we had a meeting at CBS.

Then I sat in on the writer pitching the script, and I pitched a fit!

This was a mistake. A wrong move.

Then I heard Barbara Branden was pitching a fit!

She hated the script.

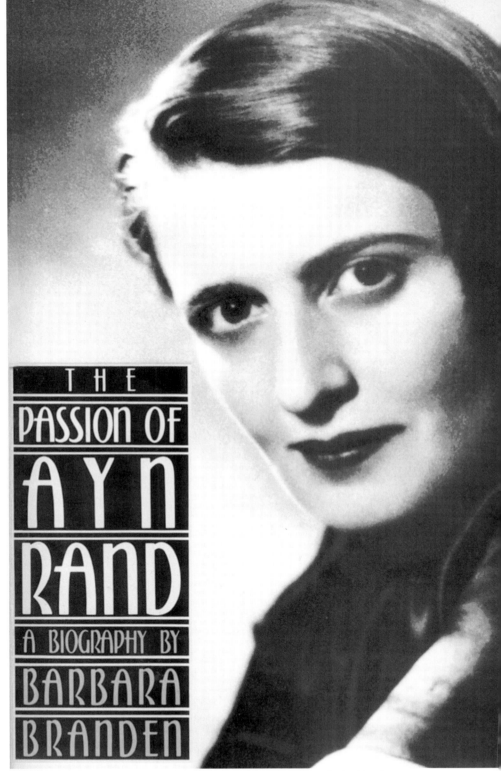

From *The Passion of Ayn Rand* by Barbara Branden, © 1986 by permission of Doubleday, a division of Random House, Inc.

Barbara had renewed my option agreement twice, and D-day was coming fast. Suddenly I received a frantic phone call from Irwin on the eve of the day my option would run out.

"Barbara won't speak to me," he panicked.

"Why?"

"She hates the script and doesn't want to go further. I begged her for four more weeks. I told her we have Showtime wanting it!" He shouted.

"Is this going to happen?" I asked.

"Ninety-nine percent sure." He said.

"I'll call her." I assured him.

Barbara was now living in Winnipeg, Manitoba, stricken with lung cancer. (Thank the Lord she is now better.)

She took my call. We had a very serious conversation about what Hollywood would do to Ayn Rand and she wanted no part of it, not for any amount of money, she said. She realized how much work I had put into it, but at this point, she said, she'd rather forget the whole thing than to have Ayn turn over in her grave. She did not want Ayn to be dismantled or misunderstood in Hollywood terms. We spoke for over an hour.

I could not convince her to give me just a few more days. We were on the brink of a deal for the project, I told her. I would guarantee that the script would be rewritten, that she'd be hired as consultant. But she could not be swayed. She expressed appreciation for all my efforts, especially the day I arranged for her to meet Anne Bancroft, who would have been perfect to play Ayn Rand.

I called Irwin and told him I couldn't persuade her to give us another forty-eight minutes much less forty-eight hours. "She was adamant," I told him.

"Can't you call Showtime and tell them the option is over at midnight tonight and if they want it, they must deliver the money?!"

"I've done that."

"Do it again!" I demanded.

"I'll try…stay by the phone."

9:00 P.M. 10:00 P.M. Then 11:00 P.M. the phone rang. It was Irwin.

"The president of Showtime just called, can you believe it? He will write the check if we partner with them on the $80,000."

"So will you partner?" He asked.

"You know, Irwin, I already have five years into it with a lot of money in the mill." I responded.

"I know, I know. I'll get back to you."

He sounded impatient.

11:15 P.M., and the phone rang.

"Here's the deal. I'll match Showtime with $40,000 if you put up $20,000 for the rewrite."

"I'll do it!" I responded.

Irwin sent a dispatch to Barbara's entertainment lawyer's home at 11:55 P.M. (five minutes before the option ran out). He rang the bell and handed the check for $80,000 over to her.

The lawyer, knowing that her client, Barbara, had made up her mind against the project, said, "You fucking bastard," instead of "Thank you," as she accepted the check and smiled.

The movie biz. It's rough out there. Cliff-hangers, all.

We shepherded this project to fruition with Showtime. Helen Mirren took the role of Ayn Rand. Peter Fonda played her husband, and Eric Stoltz was her young lover, Nathanial Branden. *The Passion of Ayn Rand* aired in 1998. Helen Mirren was nominated for the Emmy, the Golden Globe, and the Screen Actors Guild Awards. She won the Emmy. She looked and sounded as close to Ayn Rand as was humanly possible. She was brilliant. Peter Fonda was also nominated three times, and won the Golden Globe. Showtime threw an elegant party for the cast and stars of some of their other shows at L'Orangerie, a perfectly beautiful restaurant, after the event, and it felt so good. Jodie Foster was there, among many others.

OUR SON, THE CHEF

David's first chore was to cut the eyes out of the soft-shell crabs. "They died in my hands." He remembers sadly. That was his very first chore handed out by the chef at the time. (As in "So, you wanna be a chef, do you…? Well, let's see how you like this!")

FROM DAVID THE CHEF TO MOM:

"He could have asked me to clean all the green leaf lettuces, but instead I think he wanted to test me, so I got the crabs. I took a deep breath and didn't complain. Then you, Mom, made up a notebook for me detailing all the stations that I would have to learn. I was to work in each one for three weeks. There were five stations in all: Grill, Sauté, Pasta, Pantry, and Prep. Prep was daunting because there were so many things to learn. Only after I mastered all of these stations could I stand up to 'expediting,' which means to get the food out while it's hot. You instilled an attitude of exactitude in me, and a respect for the recipe and the way food was made.

"The first dish you taught me was Osso Bucco, because the chef we had embarrassed you once by serving 'tough hockey pucks' at a dinner party you gave at the restaurant. So we fast-forwarded our learning process to Osso Bucco and Lamb Shanks.

"I learned braising and sweating techniques, sauce reduction and lots of little details like mixing the seasoned flour with your hands to fluff it up and redistribute the seasonings after you roll each piece of veal in the flour. I never got lazy on those details.

"Then we did the mother sauces, and I learned how you can branch off of any one of them to make a different sauce. We watched videos together, and we also drove to faraway places to attend cooking classes.

"One day, I got the feeling that I was ready and I could do it. And you made me Executive Chef.

"If you remember, I was embarrassed by the title and I couldn't, in all honesty, step up to the plate until I had earned my stripes. Now I feel good about myself (even though you never stop learning) and I still look to you for my most honest and fair critiques. I understand mouth-feel, textures, and garnishes, and how to taste for the subtle under-flavors. During the process I got cranky and I got tired, and sometimes my ego was a problem. It was all your patient training that helped me through it. Sometimes I am still overwhelmed. As far as a palate is concerned, you really have to develop that on your own. I've gone from bland to over-salting. Now I've got it just right. Thanks, Mom."

HIGH-PROFILE THAI LAMB WITH PEPPERS AND GINGER

SERVES 6

Major Hollywood studios take over Kate Mantilini's or the Gardens on Glendon from time to time, after they preview their latest film. At Kate's, we are very near the Academy theater and just down the street from the Writers Guild theater. This dish is a great hit at such parties. They like high-profile tastes. They like high-profile everything!

❦ IN A LARGE BAKING DISH, COMBINE:

3/4 CUP BEEF BROTH OR BOUILLON

3 TABLESPOONS SOY SAUCE

continued   High-Profile Thai Lamb with Peppers and Ginger

3 TABLESPOONS MINCED FRESH GINGER

9 LITTLE DRIED RED CHILES, SEEDS REMOVED AND CRUMBLED

6 TABLESPOONS FINELY CHOPPED CILANTRO

❦ ADD TO THE MARINADE:

1 $^1/_2$ POUNDS BONELESS LAMB LOIN, SLICED ACROSS GRAIN

    INTO BITE SIZE PIECES

The lamb must be very tender, so talk to your butcher and try to buy well aged meat.

❦ COMBINE AND SET ASIDE IN A BOWL:

1 $^1/_2$ CUPS SLIVERED OR JULIENNED RED ONION

1 $^1/_2$ CUPS JULIENNED RED BELL PEPPER

2 TABLESPOONS SEEDED AND FINELY CHOPPED JALAPEÑO

    CHILE PEPPERS*

2 TABLESPOONS THINLY SLICED, PEELED FRESH GINGER, JULIENNED

❦ IN A DEEP SKILLET OR LARGE POT, HEAT:

$^1/_2$ CUP PEANUT OIL

❦ DRAIN LAMB WELL (RESERVING MARINADE) AND ADD TO
SKILLET. SAUTÉ FOR 2 MINUTES, THEN ADD THE RESERVED
VEGETABLES. SAUTÉ UNTIL CRISP-TENDER AND ADD THE
RESERVED MARINADE. COOK, STIRRING, FOR 5 TO 7 MINUTES,
UNTIL THE LAMB IS MEDIUM RARE.

❦ ADD TO PAN AND COOK FOR 1 MINUTE MORE:

SCANT $^1/_2$ CUP HOISIN SAUCE

3/4 CUP FINELY CHOPPED CILANTRO

❦ SERVE OVER RICE, OR WITH SOFT TACOS. OR SERVE A SMALL
MOUND SURROUNDED BY PICKLED VEGETABLES AND CRISPY
DEEP-FRIED WONTON QUARTERS.

* WEAR PLASTIC GLOVES WHILE WORKING WITH THESE PEPPERS —
DO NOT TOUCH YOUR EYES — I SPEAK FROM EXPERIENCE.

Kate's was getting crowded with family. David was now wearing his white chef coat tucked into his checkered chef trousers, looking very tall and hoping for the reactions and compliments due to him for a good new dish he would offer. And he *was* deserving of all the praise he received. But that's what chefs do. They need to know.

I gave him George Lang's splendid "Rules of the Chef," first printed in *Restaurant Hospitality,* January 1977:

> The Chef is always right.
>
> The Chef doesn't sleep, he rests.
>
> The Chef doesn't eat, he nourishes himself.
>
> The Chef doesn't drink, he tastes.
>
> The Chef is never late, he is delayed.
>
> The Chef never leaves the service, he is called away.
>
> If you suggest your ideas to the Chef, you will leave with his.
>
> The Chef is always the Chef even in his swimming costume.
>
> If you criticize the Chef, you criticize the almighty.

The Gardens was no longer ours. It sold with the whole company. Buying back Kate's to give Harry a base was wise. But now it was apparent that with Adam, we needed more than one base. David was fine at Kate's, cooking away. Adam became director of operations. Harry was present at every lunch and every dinner. Everyone was inundated with "the family." I knew we were going to have to spread this out. The beautiful Gardens had been the Jewel in the Crown, and I was longing to have it back. The Harvard MBA and his company who had bought all our restaurants would not give it up. They liked it too. Year after year I pursued this matter. Eight years passed, and finally they had a crisis and we were able to buy it back. Don't ask how, it's a long story. Then we could spread out and stop driving each other crazy.

David was getting raves in *Gourmet* magazine (in July 1996). Arlene Walsh at the much-read local journal *Beverly Hills 213* was an influential fan. Adam traveled between Kate's and the Gardens (four miles apart) and our guests all loved him. *His father's son.* Harry visited Kate's and the Gardens almost every lunch, and both again at dinner. This made him happy. He got (and still gets) to see all his customers and friends and hear the applause on how good everything was. And I got to work with Chef Robert of the Gardens again. The little ficus tree had grown thirty feet high and was in fine condition. What a tree! It was very soothing to us. It had been Hamlet Gardens, but the Hamlets were no longer ours. We renamed the Gardens: the Gardens on Glendon.

CLASS REUNION 1997.

WE ALL MET AT KATE'S FOR BREAKFAST ONE SUNDAY MORNING. MOST EVERYONE STARTED WITH US IN THE '50S, AND THEY ARE STILL BEAUTIFUL AND FULL OF FIRE FORTY YEARS LATER!

back row left to right HARRY, MARILYN, DAVID, VERN, DAVID, ADAM **center row** MOM, EVONNE, WARREN, HILDA, LAURO, AMY, GLORIA, ARTHUR **front row** EMMA, JOHN, WILLIAM, ANN, HILDA, ESTHER, MARVIN AND LIL

THE GARDENS'
LAVENDER PEPPER
FENNEL STEAK

SERVES 2

❧ SEASON WITH AN EVENLY SPREAD PINCH OF KOSHER SALT ON
   EACH SIDE:
   1 (12-OUNCE) TRIMMED NEW YORK STRIP STEAK, OR RIBEYE

❧ BRUSH EACH SIDE WITH:
   A. 1. STEAK SAUCE

❧ AND SPRINKLE WITH A MIXTURE OF:
   1 TEASPOON COARSELY GROUND WHITE PEPPERCORNS
   1 TEASPOON COARSELY GROUND BLACK PEPPERCORNS
   1 TEASPOON GROUND FENNEL
   1/2 TEASPOON DRIED LAVENDER FLOWERS

❧ GRILL OR SAUTÉ FOR 2 TO 3 MINUTES ON EACH SIDE,
   OR UNTIL DONE AS YOU LIKE IT. ALLOW IT TO REST FOR
   2 MINUTES, AND SERVE ON A HEATED PLATE.

"MARILYN, ARE YOU SURE YOU CAN COOK?" HE ASKED

JUST A LITTLE TIRED

What a luxury to be able to be "just a little tired" and know everything is being taken care of just the way we would have done it. We waited a very long time for this.

Each day, I found I had just enough time of my very own to rezone. *To be a little selfish about your own time is hard to do when you've never done it.*

Adding golf and swimming to my regime proved to be quite wonderful. Otherwise, the tension gets to me and eats me up alive, manifesting itself into one digestive disturbance after another. I didn't want to be doctoring all the time, and I found that having physical activity in my life made the difference. So, some personal boundaries had to go up.

I learned boundaries from our two sons, who after they were married, and even now, drew their lines in the sand so they could feel a sense of peace. If you're going to be in business together as a family, this is Lesson Number One. Draw the lines and respect them. Everyone needs their time off. Everyone needs their sense of space—but not from Harry. I want to finally hold Harry's hand.

"What'er the Course, the End Is the Renown."

—All's Well That Ends Well

My mind is like a kite in a gale wind, and I hang on to the string for dear life. What a ride it is. At every turn, I wonder if reincarnation really exists. Otherwise, how did all this happen? There is no reason in this world for me to know so much about what I am doing unless I did it somewhere else at some other time. If this might be true, then we're damned lucky to be plugged into the wisdom from someone else's life. We're blessed, especially if it turns out well.

There were times when I wondered, "Who in the hell is this? Am I supposed to know what to do here?" But there were many angels, and there is always hope.

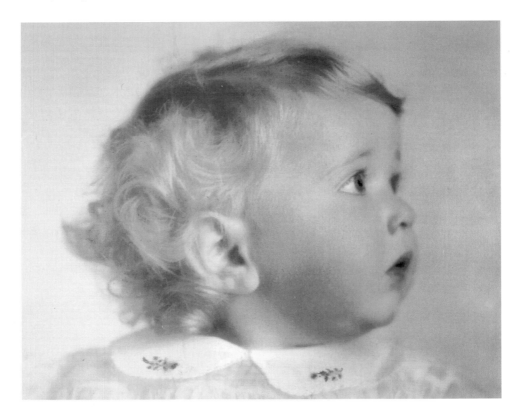